# the make-ahead
# sauce
# solution

## ELEVATE YOUR EVERYDAY MEALS
*with 61 Freezer-Friendly Sauces*

Elisabeth Bailey

Storey Publishing

The mission of Storey Publishing is to serve our customers by
publishing practical information that encourages
personal independence in harmony with the environment.

Edited by Carleen Madigan and Sarah Guare
Art direction and book design by Alethea Morrison
Text production by Jennifer Jepson Smith
Indexed by Christine R. Lindemer, Boston Road Communications
Cover and interior photography by © Joseph De Leo Photography, except
    pages 26, 28, 31, 35, 37, 40, 45, 47, 55, 58, 66, 77, 78, 87, 92, 102, 105, 107, 109,
    120, 123, 141, 143, 151, 159, 161, 172, 174, 177 and 184 by Mars Vilaubi

Storey books are available for special premium and promotional uses and for customized editions. For further information, please call 800-793-9396.

**Storey Publishing**
210 MASS MoCA Way
North Adams, MA 01247
storey.com

Printed in China by Toppan Leefung
    Printing Ltd.
10 9 8 7 6 5 4 3 2 1

LIBRARY OF CONGRESS CATALOGING-IN-PUBLICATION DATA

Names: Bailey, Elisabeth, author.
Title: The make-ahead sauce solution : elevate your everyday meals with 61 freezer-friendly sauces / Elisabeth Bailey.
Description: North Adams, MA : Storey Publishing, [2018] | Includes index.
Identifiers: LCCN 2018000664 (print) | LCCN 2018001542 (ebook) | ISBN 9781612129600 (ebook) | ISBN 9781612129594 (pbk. : alk. paper)
Subjects: LCSH: Sauces. | Make-ahead cooking. | LCGFT: Cookbooks.
Classification: LCC TX819.A1 (ebook) | LCC TX819.A1 B28 2018 (print) | DDC 641.81/4—dc23
LC record available at https://lccn.loc.gov/2018000664

# Contents

# Discover the Magic of Make-Ahead Sauces

Let me set the scene.

It's 5:00 (or 5:30 or 6:00) and you just got home from work. You are tired. You are hungry. Your kid/spouse/parent is hungry. And crabby. And has to go to an activity/do homework/do more work/get ready for tomorrow. Are you going to pull fresh vegetables and meat out of the fridge and create something healthy and inventive from scratch?

No. No, you are not. Not even if you have fresh meat and vegetables in the fridge and the time to cook them. Because you are tired.

I know because I'm tired, too. If somebody magically cooked all that gorgeous fresh food in my kitchen and put it in front of me, I'd eat it happily. If not . . . I'm going to eat whatever is easiest to make and easiest to please these other people *demanding things* at my table. Like a frozen lasagna or — yes, I'm going there — chicken nuggets and fries.

At least, that's what I used to do all the time. Now, more often than not, I've got a better solution. I've worked out a system in which someone does magically cook all that gorgeous fresh food and has it ready when I get home from work. That person is . . . Weekend Me!

On the weekend, when I have time to cook and the energy to feel like cooking, I make a big batch of something — usually a sauce. If I'm ambitious, I might even make a couple of big batches of sauce. Then I divide the sauce into meal-size batches and pop them in the freezer.

I call these sauces "flavor bombs." On a weekday night, I add any of them to a basic staple like a chicken breast, pasta, or baked potato — which I've cooked quickly and easily — and voilà! I've made a delicious, homemade meal with the same amount of energy and forethought I'd give a frozen pizza.

One of my favorite parts of this method is that you don't even need a chest freezer. Once you've built up a library of these sauces, you can easily mix and match with different staples to make a variety of meals on a moment's notice.

Please keep in mind that while terrific, this method isn't likely to be a 100 percent solution to your weekday dinner dilemma. It certainly hasn't prevented processed food from ever entering my kitchen! Don't aim for perfection. If you use this book to structure half your meals, that's a big success. If more, that's even better. Think of every home-cooked meal as a victory, and give yourself an extra pat on the back for successfully mixing and matching bases and sauces. You aren't just succeeding at cooking — you're laying a foundation for creating your own bases and sauces in the future.

Sound good? Okay, let's get down to the nitty-gritty.

## The Method

My recipes basically consist of two parts, which you can mix and match: the bases, which are easy staples you make on a weekday night, and the sauces, which take more time and are made on weekends and frozen. Many of my sauces are rich with vegetables, and for those that aren't, it's a good idea to have some prepared vegetables to serve on the side. Those sides you can simply pull from the freezer and heat (see Veggies on the Side, page 22).

One of the advantages to making sauces on weekends and freezing them is that you have months, rather than days, to enjoy the fruits of your labor. Sauces that don't contain dairy will keep very well in the freezer for up to 6 months; those that do have dairy should be used within 1 month.

## Freezing 101

After you've cooked your food, it's very important to cool it in the refrigerator before transferring it to containers for freezing. This prevents condensation, which will freeze into ice crystals and affect the taste of your food.

### Bag It!

After your food is cool, I recommend that you freeze foods flat in freezer bags to maximize your freezer space. Unlike hard-sided plastic containers, bags waste no space while keeping air away from food. Good-quality freezer bags are also reusable — wash them out just like you would a hard-sided container, air-dry, and reuse. One quick caveat: If you happen to have a chest freezer with oodles of space for sauce or would prefer to use different containers, go for it! The recipes in this book can be frozen in any freezer-safe container you wish to use.

When shopping for supplies, choose BPA-free, resealable plastic bags that are labeled "freezer bags." You'll want a selection of sizes — gallon, quart, and pint. Most sauces for most families will be frozen in gallon bags, while quart bags are best for some of the more compact sauces as well as meals for smaller families. Pint bags are usually best for single servings. I often make a big batch of sauce, then I fill a few gallon bags for family meals as well as pint bags for lunches. If you have a picky eater in your family, consider freezing single portions just for that person — you can easily heat up an individual portion of a mild tomato sauce, for instance, while everyone else has a more adventuresome option.

## FREEZER BAG SIZES

| TYPE | SIZE | CAPACITY | MAX. AMOUNT OF SAUCE |
| --- | --- | --- | --- |
| Pint | Small | 2 cups | 1½ cups |
| Quart | Medium | 4 cups | 3 cups |
| Gallon | Large | 16 cups | 12 cups |

Because different bases require different amounts of sauce, you may wish to think through which bases you plan to serve and freeze the exact amounts of sauce you will need for each dinner. For instance, my family loves to eat All-Around Vegetable sauce (page 41) over either baked potatoes or chicken. We usually eat a total of four baked potatoes for dinner and I need 1 cup of sauce per potato, so I label a gallon bag "All-Around Vegetable Sauce for Potatoes — 4 servings" and fill it with 4 cups of sauce. Since I usually cook 2 pounds of chicken at a time (one for dinner that night and one to heat up later in the week) and I need 1½ cups of sauce per pound of chicken, I also label a quart bag for chicken and fill it with 3 cups of sauce.

**Filling bags.** It pays to be cautious when transferring sauce to a freezer bag! If you're holding a plastic bag with one hand and a ladle with the other, you're asking for a frustrating mess. Instead, I recommend following the method on the next page.

## How to Fill Bags with Sauce

1. Place your plastic bag inside a wide-mouth jar. When in doubt, choose the larger bag.

2. Place a wide funnel on top of the bag.

3. Ladle your sauce into a measuring cup, then pour the sauce slowly through the wide funnel into the bag. Fill the bag no more than three-quarters full, both for ease of use and to allow room for liquids to expand as they freeze (see Freezer Bag Sizes, page 3).

*Sealing bags.* After you're done filling the bags, remove as much air as possible. If you are serious about freezing, you can always purchase a vacuum sealer, such as a FoodSaver. If you don't have a vacuum sealer, you can use one of two methods: For bags that contain meat or other foods that might pose a health hazard, submerge the bags in a bowl of water (see below). For all other foods, use a straw to suck out the air (see page 6).

## Bowl-of-Water Method for Sealing Bags

1. Submerge the open bag in the water, keeping the open edge just above the surface. The pressure of the water will push out the air and mold the bag around the food.

2. Seal the bag quickly and remove from the water. Be sure to dry the outside of the bag thoroughly before freezing.

## Straw Method for Sealing Bags

1. Insert the straw into the corner of a bag and seal the bag as much as possible.

2. Suck out the air through the straw until you see the bag collapse around the contents of the bag.

3. While still maintaining suction, pull out the straw and quickly seal the rest of the bag.

## Freezer Storage Tips

If you give your freezer a good clean-out before you start cooking sauces, you should be able to store as many as 30 family meals' worth of sauces in the freezer compartment of your refrigerator. To get each bag perfectly flat and to prevent them from sticking to each other, lay sheets of cardboard between them.

**Organize everything.** After bags are completely frozen, store similar items together. Stand them vertically in labeled plastic shoe boxes or other small plastic containers. Make dairy its own category, since you'll need to use those sauces more quickly.

**Date, label, and rotate!** While the freezer will keep foods for long periods of time, they won't keep forever, even in tightly sealed bags. Whenever you add new food to the freezer, slot it into the back of the box so that the older food is to the front. Do a clean-out every 6 months. Is there anything in your freezer that you've looked at and thought, "Well, sometime — but not tonight" for 6 months or longer? Sometime is not going to happen. Time to toss it.

*Sheets of cardboard prevent bags from sticking together. Now these bags are ready for vertical storage.*

## Thawing and Reheating

It's best to allow sauces to defrost in the fridge, but you can also go from freezer to stove. If you think of it, place the sauce in the fridge either the evening before or the morning of the day you'll be using it. When you're ready to make dinner, simply pour the sauce from the bag into a saucepan and warm over medium heat until it is hot throughout. If the sauce is still frozen, transfer it from the bag to a saucepan and warm over low heat, stirring gently but often, until the sauce is thawed. Then increase the heat to medium and finish heating.

## WHAT IF . . .

**The power goes out.** Don't panic. Leave your freezer door closed. The food should stay safe for 24 hours, especially if the freezer is full! If your power is out for more than a full day, however, I'm afraid you'll lose the contents.

**I didn't finish the sauce. Can I refreeze it?** Yes, but make sure you heat the unused portion to a simmer, and *then* refreeze it to make sure you kill off any bacteria it may have picked up along the way.

**It looks funny when I reheat it.** Depending on the quality of your freezer and how often the door is opened, some sauces may change texture slightly after being frozen and reheated. Those that contain dairy products can be especially tricky. Expect that sauces containing yogurt or sour cream will change texture slightly — this does not mean they've gone bad! When in doubt, test it. As you are reheating your sauce, give it a few big whiffs. Does it smell okay? If so, wait until the sauce is at a simmer, and then sample it. Does it taste good? Great — you're fine. If it doesn't smell or taste right, dump it.

# Preparing a Base for Your Sauce

In the following pages, I lay out my favorite preparation method for each base for a busy weekday night. If you are a less experienced cook or just want to do the simplest thing, you may want to follow the base recipes to a T, but you don't need to. The sauces are designed to work with a variety of preparation methods, so if you prefer whole roasted chicken to pan-fried chicken breasts, by all means roast your chicken. Or simply purchase one preroasted from the deli counter. Use mashed potatoes instead of baked if you wish, or pork chops instead of tenderloin . . . you get the picture.

After each sauce recipe, I give a list of the bases I recommend for that sauce, including my personal favorite base. Some bases will make for a heavier meal than others, and some sauces are heavier than others, so take that into account when selecting which recipes to try.

# Pasta

Pasta makes a quick and satisfying meal. Wait until the sauce is close to ready before starting your pasta, so you can immediately add the cooked pasta to a finished sauce and serve. Use enough water to allow the pasta to move about freely — cramming too much pasta into too small a pot is a common mistake.

1. Bring a large pot of cold water to a rapid boil. Add a generous pinch of salt (as if you were seasoning a pot of soup) before adding the pasta. Do not add oil or butter to the water because it will interfere with the sauce's ability to stick to the pasta.

2. Immediately after adding the pasta to the boiling water, give it a stir. Continue to stir often as it cooks. Use the time on the package as a guide; start checking the pasta for doneness 1 or 2 minutes before the prescribed cooking time. The pasta is done when it is tender but slightly firm.

*Don't cook different sizes of pasta in the same pot, as they won't cook evenly.*

3. Remove the pasta from the heat and drain it in a colander. Reserve 1 cup of the cooking liquid to thin the sauce, if desired.

4. Immediately after draining the pasta, add the pasta to the sauce, rather than the other way around. This discourages pieces of pasta from sticking together. If you will be using the pasta for a cold pasta salad, rinse it under cold water just after draining to arrest the cooking process.

## THE RIGHT SHAPE

Shaped or tubed pastas (like penne, macaroni, or rigatoni) are good with chunky sauces or sauces with heavy cheeses, like Sausage Ragu (page 127) or Cheddar Ale (page 134). Long, thin pastas (like spaghetti, fettucine, and linguine) were designed to hold oily and creamy sauces in pleasing proportions. They are the best choice for sauces such as Vodka Cream Sauce (page 96) or Gorgonzola Chive Butter (page 137).

# Baked Potatoes

A baked potato is one of my favorite bases. It takes a bit more time to cook than other bases, but the cooking requires little effort on your part.

Different kinds of potatoes have different textures, depending on the density of their flesh. I recommend sticking to russets — they have a fluffy texture that's a perfect vehicle for many of the sauces in this book, and they bake beautifully. One large russet per person is an easy foundation for a meal.

1. Preheat the oven to 425°F/220°C. Line a baking sheet with parchment paper or aluminum foil.

2. Scrub the potatoes clean under running water and dry with a dishcloth or paper towel. If you plan to eat the skins, rub each potato with 1 or 2 teaspoons of olive oil, and season with salt and pepper to taste.

3. Stab each potato in three or four places with a fork. This allows steam to escape and minimizes the possibility that a potato will explode in your oven or in your face (it happens!).

4. Place the potatoes on the prepared baking sheet and bake for about 1 hour, or until soft inside. Split, sauce, and serve.

If you don't have an hour to cook your potatoes in the oven, you can pop them in a slow cooker first thing in the morning. Add a cup of water or broth and cook on low for 10 hours (no rack required). Or you can microwave them on high for 4 to 5 minutes per side, turning them halfway through the cooking time.

*Be sure to stab the potatoes several times before cooking.*

# Rice

There are many different varieties and types of rice, from long-grain to short-grain and from white to red to black. I recommend using basic long-grain white rice. It cooks reliably every time with the same proportions of water to rice, and it has a clean, neutral flavor. If you prefer brown rice, you may use the same preparation method described below, but cook for 45 minutes.

**1.** Combine water or broth (chicken or vegetable) with rice in a saucepan. Use 1¾ cups water or broth for every cup of rice. (One serving is about ½ cup uncooked rice.) Rice is perfectly delicious plain or with just a pinch of salt. You can add a tablespoon of butter to the uncooked rice, if desired.

**2.** Stir the ingredients, cover the pan, and bring to a boil over medium heat.

Quickly reduce the heat to low and simmer until the liquid is absorbed and the rice is cooked through but still a bit firm, about 20 minutes. Give it a taste. If it is still too firm, add a few more tablespoons of water, cover, and cook until the water is absorbed.

**3.** Remove the rice from the heat and let rest, covered, for 5 minutes before serving with sauce.

*Basic long-grain white rice cooks reliably every time and has a clean, neutral flavor.*

# Tofu

When cooking tofu, your goal should be to make it crisp and browned. To achieve this, start with the firmest tofu you can find and dry it. One 14-ounce package of tofu has roughly four servings.

1. Drain the tofu, then dry it by blotting it gently with clean dishcloths or paper towels.

2. Slice the tofu into bite-size cubes and place in a large bowl.

3. Boil 1 cup water and 1 teaspoon salt in a small saucepan. Pour the boiling salted water over the cubes, then drain immediately. It seems counterintuitive to pour water on something that you're trying to dry, but both the heat and the salt will draw moisture out of the tofu for a drier finished product.

4. Place a clean dishcloth or a couple of paper towels on a plate. Using tongs or a straining spoon, remove the cubes from the bowl and lay them on the plate. Gently blot the cubes and let them drain for 20 minutes.

5. When you are ready to cook, toss your tofu cubes with ¼ cup cornstarch in a mixing bowl. The crispy coating created by the cornstarch will allow the tofu to retain its texture even in a wet sauce, and it will also help the tofu hold flavor.

6. Line a plate with paper towels. Pan-fry the coated cubes in a generous layer of oil of your choice (I like peanut) over medium-high heat. Cook the tofu until browned and crispy, 8 to 10 minutes, then transfer to the paper towel–lined plate to drain the excess oil.

7. Toss the tofu with your sauce of choice and serve immediately.

## TOFU AND MARINADE DON'T MIX!

Under no circumstances should you marinate tofu. It may seem like a good idea because you are infusing something flavorless with flavor, but the marinade makes the tofu wet (bad) and difficult to cook through without overcooking the outside (worse). With tofu, the rule is first fry, then flavor — either with a sauce or with dry spices.

# Chicken

Even though I'm a fool for roast chicken, I hardly ever make it during the week. For a quick, next-to-no-thought meal, it's hard to beat a pan-fried piece of chicken. For that reason, I recommend using boneless, skinless breasts or thighs.

1. Cover each breast or thigh with parchment paper or plastic wrap. Using a rolling pin or meat tenderizer, flatten them to about half the original thickness. Season each piece with salt and pepper to taste and set aside.

2. Heat a cast-iron pan over medium-high heat. Add ½ tablespoon butter per breast and 1 teaspoon per thigh to quickly coat the bottom of the pan. Add the chicken and pan-fry until browned and cooked through, 5 to 7 minutes per side, turning halfway through. Test for doneness by cutting through the widest part of the chicken with a steak knife to check that there is no pinkness left and that the juices run clear.

3. Transfer the chicken to a cutting board and let cool for 5 minutes, then cut by slicing against the grain.

4. Sauce and serve.

*Chicken breasts and thighs tend to be enormously plump, so it's a good idea to flatten them for more even and predictable cooking.*

# Shrimp and Scallops

Unless you live in a coastal fishing region and can buy just-caught shrimp and scallops, I strongly recommend always purchasing them frozen because they are more fresh-tasting and nutritious.

Shrimp is one of the easiest and quickest bases to make — simply heat and serve. To save time, purchase raw shrimp peeled and deveined, if you can. Bags of frozen shrimp will have a count on them; the fewer the total count, the larger the individual shrimp, and the more expensive they are. I prefer small (size 36–45) to medium (size 31–35) frozen shrimp because they have more surface area for sauce to cling to.

Scallops are nearly as easy to use as shrimp, and they cook up in a flash. If you live in a scallop-fishing area like I do and your scallops are extra large, cut them in half to get more surface for browning (see Brown Is Good: Maillard, page 19).

1. Unlike most foods, I do not recommend allowing shrimp and scallops to thaw slowly in the refrigerator. Instead, place the frozen seafood in a colander and run cold water over it, tossing occasionally, until it defrosts, about 5 minutes. There should be no trace of ice and the meat should be soft and bendable.

2. Heat a cast-iron pan over medium-high heat. Add 1 tablespoon butter or oil for every ½ pound of raw seafood to quickly coat the bottom of the pan.

3. **For shrimp,** pan-fry, stirring often, until the shrimp lose their opacity and look thoroughly pink, about 5 minutes. Be sure to remove them from the heat before they curl up tightly and become tough.

**For scallops,** pan-fry for about 5 minutes. Do not stir the scallops, but flip them halfway through cooking. Cut one in half to test for doneness — the interior should be slightly rare (pinkish-white with a slight sheen) but not raw.

4. Sauce and serve immediately.

*Because shrimp and scallops have similar meaty qualities and generally pair with the same sauces, you can use them interchangeably, or mix them together in a single dish.*

# White Fish

White fish — such as haddock, cod, tilapia, or grouper — is milder-tasting than darker fish like salmon and tuna and therefore works better with a wide range of sauces. I generally prefer cod when I can afford it and haddock when I can't, but choose whichever white fish is affordable and appealing to you. White fish can be defrosted in the refrigerator the day you plan to cook it.

1. Whisk ½ cup fine flour (use quick-mixing flour, such as Wondra from Gold Medal, or pastry flour) with ½ teaspoon salt and ½ teaspoon freshly ground black pepper per pound of fish in a shallow bowl or on a plate.

2. Heat a cast-iron pan over medium-high heat. While the pan is heating, dredge the fillets in the flour mixture.

3. Add 1 tablespoon butter or oil to the pan, quickly swirl, then add the dredged fillets in a single layer (do not crowd; cook in batches as needed). Fry the fillets, flipping halfway through, until cooked through, 2 to 3 minutes per side. Fish is cooked through when the thickest part is white and has lost its glossy tone.

4. Transfer the cooked fish to a paper towel–lined plate for 1 minute to drain excess oil.

5. Sauce and serve immediately.

*Boneless, skinless fillets of frozen fish are the best choice.*

# Pork

My favorite cut of pork, for both its price and its ease of preparation, is the tenderloin. Pork tenderloin is reliably consistent and easy to cook. Tenderloins usually weigh between 1 and 1½ pounds each, and they're often sold in packages of two.

One of the challenges with pork is knowing when it's cooked through. It can become dry and chewy quickly if overcooked, however, so it's best to use a meat thermometer to gauge doneness.

1. Place a cast-iron pan in the oven and preheat to 450°F/230°C.

2. Combine 1 tablespoon extra-virgin olive oil and 1 teaspoon salt per tenderloin in a large bowl and stir to combine. Add the pork tenderloin and roll in the salted oil to cover thoroughly.

3. Carefully transfer the tenderloin to the preheated pan and bake for 10 minutes.

4. Remove the pan from the oven, flip the meat over, and return it to the oven. Reduce the heat to 400°F/200°C and cook for 10 minutes longer, or until a thermometer plunged into the thickest part of the tenderloin reads between 140 and 145°F/60 and 63°C. At this temperature, the meat inside may still look a bit pink, but it is cooked through.

5. Remove the pan from the oven and let the meat rest for 10 minutes. Slice, sauce, and serve! For extrathin slices on cold pork sandwiches, refrigerate after resting and slice cold.

*While beef can be left rare, pork should always be cooked completely through, with just a little pink in the middle.*

# Beef

If you're like me, you've ruined a good piece of meat once or twice by cooking it at the wrong temperature. Some cuts of beef, like lean steaks, prefer a quick treatment over high heat, while others, like roasts, do better at a lower heat for a longer time. My go-to cut of beef is sirloin tip.

1. If you have a thick cut of beef, you may wish to pound it flat. To do so, cover each piece of meat with parchment paper or plastic wrap, then, using a rolling pin or meat tenderizer, flatten it to about half the original thickness.

2. Rub the cut all over with about 1 tablespoon extra-virgin olive oil and 1 teaspoon salt per pound of meat.

*Sirloin tip can be cooked quickly over high heat in the same manner as a steak, and it is a great choice for quick, affordable weeknight dinners.*

3. Preheat a cast-iron skillet over medium-high heat. Place the beef in the skillet and cook until well seared and browned, 3 to 5 minutes per side. Reduce the heat to medium-low, cover, and cook to desired doneness. Check the meat by taking its temperature with a meat thermometer or by cutting into the thickest part with a steak knife and peeking in. Rare beef (130°F/55°C) should still be red in the middle, with pink edging and a brown exterior; medium beef (145°F/63°C) should be pink in the middle with a brown exterior; and well-done beef (160°F/71°C) should be cooked until no trace of pink remains.

4. Transfer the beef to a room-temperature surface to rest for 10 minutes, then slice, sauce, and serve.

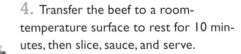

# BROWN IS GOOD: MAILLARD

No matter what you eat or how you prepare it, one of the universal food rules I like to impress upon cooks is to get brown with it. This is especially true for meats and pan-fried foods, as well as anything that can caramelize, like onions (see Brown Is Good: Caramelization, page 149). Let's take a look at why brown seems to be the color of good flavor, especially in meats.

When you brown a steak in a pan or on the grill, you are taking advantage of something called the Maillard reaction. The Maillard reaction is a chemical reaction between an amino acid and a sugar, both of which are already present in certain foods. Different amino acids cause different flavors and amounts of browning. When high heat is applied to the food, usually between 285 and 330°F/140 and 165°C, the Maillard reaction creates a number of flavor compounds that people enjoy. It is important to keep the temperature in this range so you do get browning (good!) but don't burn the exterior of the food (bad!). Experimentation and experience will teach you where to draw the line. A pressure cooker is a great tool for creating Maillard reactions with a good amount of control.

The other key trick to successful browning with the Maillard reaction is to keep your food as dry as possible, as the presence of water causes food to steam instead of brown. You can blot any moisture off the surface of your steak with a paper towel, for instance, and be sure not to crowd food in a pan regardless of what you are cooking.

Other common foods that get part of their flavor from Maillard reactions include French fries, toast, coffee, and toasted marshmallows.

# Sandwiches

This one is pretty much self-explanatory. Take a big dollop of sauce and spread it on bread, a tortilla, or your favorite bread alternative in the same way you would mustard or mayonnaise. Suggestions include Curried Spinach (page 83) on a chicken sandwich, Sun-Dried Tomato Pesto (page 166) with sliced roast beef and baby spinach, and ham and cheese with Tomatillo Salsa Cruda (page 176). Don't stop there, though — get creative with meat and veggie pairings! I most often make saucy sandwiches with baguette slices, as the crisp crust around the entire loaf helps keep moist sauces in.

# Soup

Simply thinning a sauce into soup is a ridiculously quick and easy way to make dinner. Sauces that I suggest can be served as "soup" (like Pumpkin Coconut Cream, page 39, shown below) can simply be thinned with broth, milk, cream, or a mixture of those to make a soup. Add 1 to 1½ cups liquid for every 1 cup of sauce, heat to a simmer, and serve. Ta-da!

# Veggies on the Side

Let's say you have a freezer full of sauces but feel like you're not getting quite enough veggies in your family's diet. As we've already established, nobody feels like washing, chopping, and cooking a side dish from scratch on a weekday night. Luckily, steamed vegetables freeze beautifully, are nutritional powerhouses, and take practically no time to go from freezer to table.

On the weekend, or whenever you have more free time, simply chop the vegetables into uniform, bite-size pieces. Place a steamer basket in a saucepan and add about 1 inch of water to the pan, being sure the water doesn't actually touch the basket. Bring the water to a boil, then add the vegetables. Steam the vegetables, covered, until mostly tender but still slightly crunchy (they will continue to cook internally for a bit after being removed from the heat). Here are some timing guidelines:

» **Steam root vegetables** and other dense vegetables, including carrots, potatoes, rutabaga, and winter squash, for 15 to 20 minutes.
» **Steam kale** and other sturdy greens for 10 minutes.
» **Steam medium-density vegetables** such as green beans, cauliflower, and broccoli for 7 minutes.
» **Steam peas,** spinach, and other tender greens for 3 minutes.

I strongly recommend using a timer! Minutes have a bad tendency to while themselves away in the kitchen, especially when you're working on several dishes at once.

Feel free to steam a variety of different vegetables in the same basket. Start with those that need the longest steam time first, then add others as appropriate.

Before freezing, toss the steamed vegetables with a bit of butter or olive oil, salt, and a quick squirt of lemon or lime juice. For even more flavor, add chopped fresh herbs or one of these before freezing:

» **Spicy peanut sauce:** Mix 2 tablespoons peanut butter, 1 teaspoon red pepper flakes, and ½ tablespoon peanut oil. Pour over steamed green beans, sweet potatoes, or nearly any other veggie combination you can think of.
» **Zesty herb dressing:** Combine 2 tablespoons red wine vinegar, 1 tablespoon extra-virgin olive oil, 1 teaspoon minced fresh oregano, and a pinch of salt. Try this dressing on corn, broccoli, potatoes, or a combination.

» **Sesame sauce:** *Combine 2 tablespoons toasted sesame oil with 1 tablespoon soy sauce and 1 tablespoon sesame seeds. This Asian-inspired flavor works well with both tender and hearty greens.*
» **Veggie soup:** *Pack the steamed vegetables in broth and freeze, then thaw and enjoy as a soup!*

To incorporate any of these frozen veggies into your dinner, allow them to thaw in the refrigerator during the day. Then reheat them over low heat in a covered pot, stirring often, until hot.

# CHAPTER 1

# ACROSS THE AMERICAS

From North to South America, the rich and diverse flavors of these sauces reflect the people who created them. Fittingly, they include heritage recipes as well as newer creations. The one thing they all have in common is great taste!

# Creamy Chipotle

Did you know that eating spicy food can actually help you cool down on a hot day by making you sweat? This blend-and-eat sauce is a good solution for those days when it's too hot to cook. Use it cold with a chilled base, or warm it gently and toss with hot food for a warm meal.

2 cups sour cream

3 whole chipotle chiles in adobo sauce, minced

2 garlic cloves, minced or pressed

Zest and juice of 1 lime

1. Combine the sour cream, chiles, garlic, and lime zest and juice in a blender and blend until smooth. (Alternatively, blend with an immersion blender in a mixing bowl.) Let rest for 10 minutes to allow the flavors to blend.

2. Freeze according to the directions on page 2. The sauce will keep in the freezer for up to 1 month.

3. To serve, follow the directions on page 8 to heat your sauce, then enjoy it on your choice of base at right.

# CREAMY CHIPOTLE MEALS TO MAKE

| BASE | QUANTITY | MEAL SUGGESTION |
|------|----------|-----------------|
| (page 11) | ⅔ cup sauce per potato | Spoon sauce over potato. Top with ⅓ cup shredded cheddar cheese. Serve with tomato salad. |
| (page 12) | ½ cup sauce per cup of cooked rice | Spoon sauce over rice. Top with ⅓ cup shredded Monterey Jack cheese. Serve with Greek salad. |
| (page 14) | 1 cup sauce per pound of chicken | Spoon sauce over sliced chicken. Serve with saffron rice and green salad. |
| (page 15) | 1 cup sauce per pound of shrimp/scallops | Spoon sauce over pan-fried shrimp. Serve with tortillas and roasted mixed bell peppers. |
| (page 17) | 1 cup sauce per pound of pork | Spoon sauce over sliced pork. Serve with Mexican rice and sliced mango. |
| (page 18) | 1 cup sauce per pound of beef | Spoon sauce over sliced beef. Serve with hash browns and Caesar salad. |
| (page 20) | ¼ cup sauce per sandwich | *My Family's Favorite:* Spread sauce evenly over 1 tortilla. Top with chopped chicken, shredded cheddar cheese, and sliced tomato. |

# Creole

Sometimes called "red gravy," this Louisiana staple relies upon the "holy trinity" of celery, onions, and bell peppers to lay the flavor base of the sauce. Dixie Beer works especially well in this recipe and is a great accompaniment to the meal, though any lager or pilsner will work.

1. Heat the oil in a large stockpot over medium heat. Add the celery, onions, bell peppers, Cajun spice, and salt, and sauté, stirring often, until the vegetables are soft and fragrant, 8 to 10 minutes.

2. Add the carrots, garlic, tomatoes, broth, beer, pepper flakes (if using), and bay leaves. Bring the mixture to a simmer and cook, uncovered, until the liquid is slightly reduced and the carrots are tender, about 20 minutes. Remove from the heat and add the parsley and thyme, and season generously with black pepper.

¼ cup extra-virgin olive oil

1 bunch celery stalks, diced

2 medium onions, diced

2 green bell peppers, diced

2 tablespoons Cajun spice

1 teaspoon salt

4–5 large carrots, diced

1 head garlic, cloves finely chopped

2 (28-ounce) cans diced tomatoes

4 cups chicken or vegetable broth

2 (12-ounce) bottles beer (pilsner or lager)

1–2 tablespoons red pepper flakes (optional)

2 bay leaves

2 cups chopped fresh parsley

2 tablespoons chopped fresh thyme

Freshly ground black pepper

*Recipe continues on page 30*

Pan-fried shrimp over grits
with Creole sauce

3. Cool the sauce in the refrigerator, then freeze according to the directions on page 2. The sauce will keep in the freezer for up to 6 months.

4. To serve, follow the directions on page 8 to reheat your sauce, then enjoy it on any one of the bases below.

## CREOLE MEALS TO MAKE

| BASE | QUANTITY | MEAL SUGGESTION |
| --- | --- | --- |
| (page 10) | 2 cups sauce per pound of pasta | Spoon sauce over penne. Serve with garlic toast. |
| (page 11) | 1 cup sauce per potato | Spoon sauce over potato. Top with shredded mozzarella cheese. |
| (page 12) | ¾ cup sauce per cup of cooked rice | Spoon sauce over rice. Serve with baked acorn squash. |
| (page 14) | 1½ cups sauce per pound of chicken | Spoon sauce over sliced chicken. Serve with French bread. |
| (page 15) | 1½ cups sauce per pound of shrimp/ scallops | *My Family's Favorite:* Toss pan-fried shrimp with sauce. Serve over grits. |
| (page 17) | 1½ cups sauce per pound of pork | Spoon sauce over sliced pork. Serve with corn bread. |
| (page 18) | 1½ cups sauce per pound of beef | Spoon sauce over sliced beef. Serve with hash browns. |

# Chimichurri

Colorful, flavorful, and fun to say quickly three times, chimichurri is a traditional Argentinean sauce and marinade. It pairs well with Italian food as well as Central and South American cuisines.

1 cup red wine vinegar

2 teaspoons salt

1 head garlic, cloves minced or pressed

1 large onion, finely diced

1 jalapeño, minced

1 cup fresh cilantro

½ cup fresh parsley

¼ cup fresh oregano

1½ cups extra-virgin olive oil

1. Combine the vinegar, salt, garlic, onion, and jalapeño in a medium mixing bowl. Cover and let rest for at least 20 minutes to allow the vegetables to begin pickling and the flavors to meld.

2. In the meantime, mince the cilantro, parsley, and oregano. Add the herbs to the pickling vegetables and stir to combine. Stir in the oil.

3. Freeze according to the directions on page 2. The sauce will keep in the freezer for up to 6 months.

4. To serve, follow the directions on page 8 to heat your sauce, then enjoy it on any one of the bases on the next page.

# CHIMICHURRI MEALS TO MAKE

| BASE | QUANTITY | MEAL SUGGESTION |
|------|----------|-----------------|
| (page 14) | ½ cup sauce per pound of chicken | Spoon sauce over sliced chicken. Serve with tortillas and roasted corn. |
| (page 15) | ½ cup sauce per pound of shrimp/ scallops | Spoon sauce over pan-fried scallops. Serve with corn bread and roasted mixed bell peppers. |
| (page 17) | ½ cup sauce per pound of pork | Spoon sauce over sliced pork. Serve with white rice and green salad. |
| (page 18) | ½ cup sauce per pound of beef | *My Family's Favorite:* Spoon sauce over sliced beef. Serve with French fries and tomato salad. |

*At right: Pan-fried steak with Chimichurri, French fries, and tomato salad*

# Mole

This rich Mexican dish uses nuts, spices, and chocolate to create a unique savory sauce. Different chile powders have different heat levels; choose one to suit your taste. Ancho chile powder is a good choice for people who don't want to singe their tongues!

1. Combine the raisins with ½ cup hot water in a small bowl and set aside.

2. Heat a medium, dry saucepan over medium heat. Toast the sesame and sunflower seeds, stirring constantly, until lightly toasted, about 5 minutes. Transfer the seeds to a plate or bowl. Reduce the heat to low and, in the same pan, combine the lard, chile powder, salt, cinnamon, cumin, and black pepper. Cook, stirring often, until the mixture is hot and very fragrant, 3 to 4 minutes.

3. Add the raisins with water, toasted seeds, almonds, and chocolate to the lard mixture. Stir in the broth and cook, stirring, until the chocolate is melted, 5 to 7 minutes.

4. Blend in the pan with an immersion blender, or transfer to a stand blender, purée, and return to the pan. Continue to cook, stirring often, until the mixture thickens, about 20 minutes.

¼ cup raisins

½ cup sesame seeds

¼ cup shelled sunflower seeds

¼ cup lard

2 tablespoons chile powder (cayenne, ancho, pasilla, or a combination)

1 teaspoon salt

½ teaspoon ground cinnamon

½ teaspoon ground cumin

½ teaspoon freshly ground black pepper

¼ cup ground almonds

2 ounces dark chocolate, chopped into small pieces

4 cups beef broth

5. Cool the sauce in the refrigerator, then freeze according to the directions on page 2. The sauce will keep in the freezer for up to 6 months.

6. To serve, follow the directions on page 8 to reheat your sauce, then enjoy it on your choice of base below.

## MOLE MEALS TO MAKE

| BASE | QUANTITY | MEAL SUGGESTION |
|------|----------|-----------------|
| (page 14) | 1 cup sauce per pound of chicken | *My Family's Favorite:* Spoon sauce over sliced chicken. Serve with white rice and roasted mixed bell peppers. |
| (page 17) | 1 cup sauce per pound of pork | Spoon sauce over sliced pork. Serve with tortillas and steamed corn. |
| (page 18) | 1 cup sauce per pound of beef | Spoon sauce over sliced beef. Serve with boiled potatoes and baked winter squash. |

# Chorizo Garlic

Be sure to use Mexican (not Spanish) chorizo for this dish. If you can't find it in your local grocery stores or Mexican food shops, you can make your own. Mix 4 to 5 tablespoons of chorizo spice mix (available online) with an equal amount of red wine vinegar, then mix with a pound of ground pork or beef.

4 cups milk

2 tablespoons butter

1 pound ground Mexican chorizo

¼ cup all-purpose flour

1 tablespoon chili powder

4 garlic cloves, minced or pressed

Freshly ground black pepper

1 cup chopped fresh cilantro

1. Heat the milk in a medium saucepan over low heat, stirring often, until the milk is heated through, about 10 minutes.

2. While the milk warms, heat a large pot over medium-high heat. Add the butter to quickly coat the bottom of the pan, then add the chorizo and cook, breaking it up and stirring, until the chorizo is cooked through, about 8 minutes.

3. Stir in the flour, chili powder, garlic, and pepper, and cook, stirring, until thoroughly combined, about 2 minutes. Pour in the hot milk and reduce the heat to low. Cook, stirring frequently, until the mixture begins to thicken, about 10 minutes. Remove from the heat and stir in the cilantro.

4. Cool the sauce in the refrigerator, then freeze according to the directions on page 2. The sauce will keep in the freezer for up to 1 month.

**5.** To serve, follow the directions on page 8 to reheat your sauce, then enjoy it on your choice of base below.

## CHORIZO GARLIC MEALS TO MAKE

| BASE | QUANTITY | MEAL SUGGESTION |
|---|---|---|
| (page 10) | 2 cups sauce per pound of pasta | Spoon sauce over rigatoni. Garnish with parsley. Serve with steamed zucchini. |
| (page 11) | 1 cup sauce per potato | Spoon sauce over potato and add a dollop of sour cream. Serve with green salad. |
| (page 12) | ½ cup sauce per cup of cooked rice | Spoon sauce over rice. Top with ¼ cup grated cheddar cheese. Serve with baked winter squash. |
| (page 20) | ⅓ cup sauce per sandwich | *My Family's Favorite:* Spread sauce evenly over hamburger bun with sliced cheese, as if it were a sloppy joe. |

# Pumpkin Coconut Cream

**MAKES**

**ABOUT 6 CUPS**

This Caribbean-inspired sauce is an unusual take on pumpkin — full and garlicky, with a good kick of heat. If you have some fresh pumpkin that doesn't seem sweet enough for pie, it's probably perfect to use here instead.

¼ cup extra-virgin olive oil

1 red bell pepper, diced

1 medium onion, finely chopped

Pinch of salt

1 chile (jalapeño or other), minced

3 garlic cloves, minced or pressed

2 (12-ounce) cans coconut milk

1 (15-ounce) can pumpkin purée or 2 cups home-made cooked pumpkin

1. Heat the oil in a large pot over medium heat. Add the bell pepper, onion, and salt, and sauté, stirring often, until the vegetables are soft and cooked through, 8 to 10 minutes.

2. Stir in the chile and garlic, and continue to cook, stirring, for 3 minutes longer. Add the coconut milk and pumpkin, stir to combine, reduce the heat to low, and cover. Simmer for 20 minutes.

3. Cool the sauce in the refrigerator, then freeze according to the directions on page 2. The sauce will keep in the freezer for up to 6 months.

4. To serve, follow the directions on page 8 to reheat your sauce, then enjoy it on any one of the bases on the next page.

*At left: Sliced chicken breast with Pumpkin Coconut Cream sauce, tortillas, and spinach salad*

# PUMPKIN COCONUT CREAM MEALS TO MAKE

| BASE | QUANTITY | MEAL SUGGESTION |
|---|---|---|
| (page 11) | ⅔ cup sauce per potato | Spoon sauce over potato. Serve with green salad. |
| (page 14) | I cup sauce per pound of chicken | *My Family's Favorite:* Spoon sauce over sliced chicken. Serve with tortillas and spinach salad. |
| (page 17) | I cup sauce per pound of pork | Spoon sauce over sliced pork. Serve with boiled potatoes and steamed broccoli. |
| (page 18) | I cup sauce per pound of beef | Spoon sauce over sliced beef. Serve with white rice and roasted mixed bell peppers. |
| (page 21) | 3½ cups sauce and 2½ cups chicken or vegetable broth per 4-serving pot | Garnish with chopped bell pepper. |

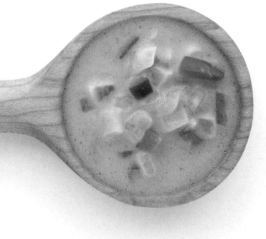

# All-Around Vegetable

This sauce serves many purposes in my home. As a vegan dish with wide appeal, it's also a good choice for emergency guest dinners. Many kids who won't touch the zucchini or peppers you use for ingredients will happily down this sauce — especially if you cover it with cheese!

½ cup extra-virgin olive oil

4 carrots, diced

3 medium onions, finely chopped

1 bunch celery (stalks only), chopped

3 green bell peppers, chopped

3 red bell peppers, chopped

2 chiles, minced (optional)

2 zucchini, finely chopped

2 sweet potatoes, diced

2 (28-ounce) cans chopped tomatoes

½ cup chopped fresh herbs (basil, parsley, sage, thyme, or a combination)

2 bay leaves

Salt and freshly ground black pepper

1. Heat the oil in a large stockpot over medium heat. Stir in the carrots, onions, celery, bell peppers, chiles (if using), zucchini, and sweet potatoes. Cover and cook, stirring occasionally, until the vegetables are just cooked through, about 15 minutes. Stir in the tomatoes, chopped herbs, and bay leaves. Cover, reduce the heat to low, and cook for 30 minutes.

2. Remove and discard the bay leaves. Purée the mixture in the pan with an immersion blender, or transfer to a stand blender, purée, and return to the pot. Add salt and black pepper to taste.

3. Cool the sauce in the refrigerator, then freeze according to the directions on page 2. The sauce will keep in the freezer for up to 6 months.

4. To serve, follow the directions on page 8 to reheat your sauce, then enjoy it on any one of the bases on page 43.

*Baked potato topped with
All-Around Vegetable sauce
and grated cheddar cheese*

# ALL-AROUND VEGETABLE MEALS TO MAKE

| BASE | QUANTITY | MEAL SUGGESTION |
|---|---|---|
| (page 10) | 2 cups sauce per pound of pasta | Spoon sauce over macaroni. Top with grated Parmesan cheese. |
| (page 11) | 1 cup sauce per potato | *My Family's Favorite:* Spoon sauce over potato. Top with ½ cup grated cheddar cheese. |
| (page 12) | ¾ cup sauce per cup of cooked rice | Spoon sauce over rice. Top with grated Havarti cheese. |
| (page 14) | 1½ cups sauce per pound of chicken | Spoon sauce over sliced chicken. Serve with biscuits. |
| (page 15) | 1½ cups sauce per pound of shrimp/scallops | Place pan-fried scallops on bed of sauce. Serve with white rice. |
| (page 16) | 1½ cups sauce per pound of fish | Spoon sauce over pan-fried fillets. Serve with wild rice blend. |
| (page 17) | 1½ cups sauce per pound of pork | Spoon sauce over sliced pork. Serve with mashed potatoes. |
| (page 18) | 1½ cups sauce per pound of beef | Spoon sauce over sliced beef. Serve with Italian bread. |
| (page 21) | 4 cups sauce and 2 cups vegetable or chicken broth or milk per 4-serving pot | Serve with oyster crackers. |

# Buffalo Sauce

MAKES

ABOUT 4 CUPS

An invention of the Anchor Bar in Buffalo, New York, buffalo sauce is traditionally served on chicken wings, but it is up to the task of spicing many different foods, including nearly any chicken or shrimp. Keep some on hand to spice up any kind of meat in a hurry. Frank's RedHot is traditionally used, but use any kind of hot sauce you like.

5 tablespoons butter

6 garlic cloves, minced or pressed

¼ cup all-purpose flour

3½ cups hot sauce

2 tablespoons white wine vinegar

1. Warm the butter in a large skillet over medium heat. Add the garlic and cook for 2 minutes, stirring often. Add the flour and stir well to combine. Continue to cook, stirring, for 5 minutes.

2. Reduce the heat to low and slowly whisk in the hot sauce, then the vinegar. Cook until the sauce thickens, about 5 minutes.

3. Cool the sauce in the refrigerator, then freeze according to the directions on page 2. The sauce will keep in the freezer for up to 6 months.

4. To serve, follow the directions on page 8 to reheat your sauce, then enjoy it on your choice of base at right.

| BASE | QUANTITY | MEAL SUGGESTION |
|---|---|---|
| (page 14) | ½ cup sauce per pound of chicken | *My Family's Favorite:* Coat chicken wings in sauce and bake at 450°F/230°C for about 45 minutes, until cooked through. Cover wings with foil for first 35 minutes, then remove. Serve with carrot sticks and blue cheese dressing and Italian bread slices. |
| (page 15) | ½ cup sauce per pound of shrimp/ scallops | Toss pan-fried shrimp with sauce. Serve with French fries and celery sticks. |
| (page 17) | ½ cup sauce per pound of pork | Spoon sauce over sliced pork. Serve with mashed potatoes and green salad. |
| (page 18) | ½ cup sauce per pound of beef | Spoon sauce over sliced beef. Serve with blue cheese dressing, white rice, and baby carrots. |
| (page 20) | 2 tablespoons sauce per sandwich | Spread sauce evenly over sandwich bun. Top with hot chicken patty and white cheddar cheese slice. |

# Green Peppercorn

Green peppercorns are the unripe version of the peppercorns we grind for black pepper. They have a clean, bright flavor over a strong burst of pure pepperiness. This bold sauce pairs best with hearty meats.

1 cup (2 sticks) butter

1 cup all-purpose flour

2 heads garlic, cloves minced or pressed

⅔ cup whole green peppercorns

1 cup vodka

1. Warm the butter in a large skillet over medium-low heat. Add the flour and cook, stirring constantly, for 4 minutes. Add the garlic and peppercorns, and cook, continuing to stir, for 2 minutes longer.

2. Stir in the vodka, cook for 5 minutes, then remove from the heat.

3. Cool the sauce in the refrigerator, then freeze according to the directions on page 2. The sauce will keep in the freezer for up to 6 months.

4. To serve, follow the directions on page 8 to reheat your sauce, then enjoy it on your choice of base at right.

# GREEN PEPPERCORN MEALS TO MAKE

| BASE | QUANTITY | MEAL SUGGESTION |
|------|----------|-----------------|
| <br>(page 10) | 1 ½ cups sauce per pound of pasta | Spoon sauce over fusilli. Top with grated Parmesan cheese. Serve with green salad. |
| <br>(page 14) | 1 cup sauce per pound of chicken | Spoon sauce over sliced chicken. Serve with white rice and steamed green beans. |
| <br>(page 17) | 1 cup sauce per pound of pork | Spoon sauce over sliced pork. Serve with baked potatoes and roasted carrots. |
| <br>(page 18) | 1 cup sauce per pound of beef | *My Family's Favorite:* Heat the sauce in the same pan you used to pan-fry tenderloin steaks, scraping the bottom with a spatula to incorporate any meaty bits. Ladle sauce over each steak and serve with Italian bread slices and tomato salad. |

# All-American Barbecue

MAKES

ABOUT 8 CUPS

This zesty, tomatoey sauce is another family favorite at my house. As with many tomato-based sauces, I find it tastes better prepared with canned tomatoes than with fresh. Certain children (who shall remain nameless) have been known to eat an entire batch with French fries.

½ cup (1 stick) butter

4 medium onions, finely diced

10-12 garlic cloves, minced

2 (28-ounce) cans diced roasted tomatoes

¼ cup brown sugar

¼ cup minced fresh cilantro

¼ cup chili powder

1 tablespoon ground cayenne pepper (optional)

2 teaspoons ground cumin

Salt and freshly ground black pepper

1. Warm the butter in a large stockpot over medium-high heat. Add the onions and sauté until tender, about 8 minutes.

2. Add the garlic and sauté for 2 minutes.

3. Stir in the tomatoes, sugar, cilantro, chili powder, cayenne (if using), cumin, and salt and pepper to taste. Bring to a boil, then reduce the heat to medium-low and simmer uncovered, stirring occasionally, for 40 minutes.

4. Cool the sauce in the refrigerator, then freeze according to the directions on page 2. The sauce will keep in the freezer for up to 6 months.

5. To serve, follow the directions on page 8 to reheat your sauce, then enjoy it on any one of the bases on page 50.

**At right:** *Ribs coated with All-American Barbecue sauce, with corn on the cob*

# ALL-AMERICAN BARBECUE MEALS TO MAKE

| BASE | QUANTITY | MEAL SUGGESTION |
| --- | --- | --- |
| (page 14) | I cup sauce per pound of chicken | Spoon sauce over sliced chicken. Serve with French fries and steamed corn. |
| (page 17) | I cup sauce per pound of pork | Spoon sauce over sliced pork. Serve with grits and green salad. |
| (page 18) | I cup sauce per pound of beef | Spoon sauce over sliced beef. Serve with biscuits and Caesar salad. |
| (page 20) | ¼ cup sauce per sandwich | Spread sauce evenly over hamburger bun. Top with cooked burger and slice of cheddar cheese. Serve with roasted mixed bell peppers. |

## ALL-AMERICAN MEAL

My family's favorite way to eat All-American Barbecue sauce is with ribs. Coat a rack of pork ribs in sauce and bake in a roasting pan at 300°F/150°C for about 2½ hours, until the meat is nearly falling off the bone. Cover the ribs with heavy-duty foil for the first 2 hours, then remove it to finish. Serve with corn on the cob.

# Anaheim Pepper

MAKES

ABOUT 5½ CUPS

Even though these chiles are named after a city in California, they originated in New Mexico. Immature green chiles are spicier than the ripe red version. If this thick, pungent sauce is too spicy for you, try a blend of red and green chiles in your next batch.

- 16 green Anaheim chiles, cored, seeded, and cut into strips
- ¾ cup extra-virgin olive oil
- 16 garlic cloves, roughly chopped
- ½ teaspoon salt
- ¾ cup heavy cream
- 1 cup finely chopped fresh cilantro

  Freshly ground black pepper

1. Position an oven rack just below the broiler. Preheat the broiler. Line a baking sheet with parchment paper.

2. Toss the chile strips with 2 tablespoons of the oil in a large mixing bowl. Arrange the strips, skin side up, on the prepared baking sheet, making sure that the strips are flat enough to avoid direct contact with the broiler element. Do not overlap them.

3. Broil the chiles for 10 to 15 minutes, depending on the thickness of the strips, until the skins are charred and the flesh is limp. Remove from the oven and set aside to cool.

4. In the meantime, heat the remaining ½ cup plus 2 tablespoons oil in a small skillet over medium heat. Add the garlic and salt, and sauté, stirring often, until the garlic is soft, about 3 minutes.

5. Once the chile strips are cool enough to touch, remove the charred skins by hand. Chop the remaining flesh into small pieces.

*Recipe continues on page 53*

Anaheim Pepper sauce on sliced chicken, with hash browns and fresh tomatoes

52

6. Combine the chopped chiles, the garlic with all the oil, and the cream, cilantro, and black pepper to taste in a blender and pulse until smooth.

7. Cool the sauce in the refrigerator, then freeze according to the directions on page 2. The sauce will keep in the freezer for up to 1 month.

8. To serve, follow the directions on page 8 to reheat your sauce, then enjoy it on your choice of base below.

## ANAHEIM PEPPER MEALS TO MAKE

| BASE | QUANTITY | MEAL SUGGESTION |
| --- | --- | --- |
| (page 10) | 1½ cups sauce per pound of pasta | Spoon sauce over shell pasta. Serve with steamed green peas. |
| (page 11) | ⅔ cup sauce per potato | Spoon sauce over potato. Serve with green salad. |
| (page 12) | ½ cup sauce per cup of cooked rice | Spoon sauce over rice. Top with crumbled bacon. Serve with baby carrots. |
| (page 14) | 1 cup sauce per pound of chicken | *My Family's Favorite:* Spoon sauce over sliced chicken. Serve with hash browns and sliced fresh tomatoes. |
| (page 17) | 1 cup sauce per pound of pork | Spoon sauce over sliced pork. Serve with biscuits and pan-fried onions. |
| (page 18) | 1 cup sauce per pound of beef | Spoon sauce over sliced beef. Serve with couscous and sliced tomatoes. |
| (page 21) | 3½ cups sauce and 2½ cups broth or milk per 4-serving pot | Serve topped with crumbled bacon, pan-fried tortilla strips, or both. |

# Bacon Gravy

This rich gravy is just as good for dinner as it is for breakfast. I recommend draining most of the grease after you fry or oven-bake the bacon, then use the "dirtiest" grease in the recipe. Make sure you dig up all the little brown bits off the bottom of the bacon pan.

12–15 strips bacon
¼ cup all-purpose flour
1 teaspoon paprika
½ teaspoon salt
4 cups milk
Freshly ground black pepper

1. Add the bacon to a large skillet and cook over medium heat until crisp, about 7 minutes. Remove the bacon and leave ¼ cup of bacon grease in the skillet. Crumble the bacon and set aside.

2. Add the flour, paprika, and salt to the bacon grease to make a roux. Cook, stirring with a spatula, until the mixture starts to brown, about 5 minutes.

3. Whisk in the milk to combine. Reduce the heat to low and cook, stirring, until the gravy starts to thicken, about 4 minutes. Remove from the heat and add the crumbled bacon and pepper to taste.

4. Cool the gravy in the refrigerator, then freeze according to the directions on page 2. The sauce will keep in the freezer for up to 1 month.

5. To serve, follow the directions on page 8 to reheat your gravy, then enjoy it on your choice of base at right.

# BACON GRAVY MEALS TO MAKE

| BASE | QUANTITY | MEAL SUGGESTION |
|------|----------|-----------------|
| (page 11) | ¾ cup gravy per potato | Spoon gravy over potato. Season liberally with pepper. Serve with tomato salad. |
| (page 12) | ⅓ cup gravy per cup of cooked rice | Spoon gravy over rice. Serve with roasted mushrooms. |
| (page 14) | 1 cup gravy per pound of chicken | Spoon gravy over sliced chicken. Serve with white rice and steamed okra. |
| (page 18) | 1 cup gravy per pound of beef | Spoon gravy over sliced beef. Serve with hash browns and roasted Brussels sprouts. |
| (page 20) | 2 tablespoons gravy per sandwich | *My Family's Favorite:* Heat gravy and ladle over fresh split biscuits or buns. Serve with sliced fresh tomato. |

# CHAPTER 2

# ASIAN INSPIRED

Spicy, delicate, savory, sweet — Asian flavor profiles run the gamut. Many of these sauces are particularly intense and can be used sparingly. Because dairy foods are rarely used in Asian cuisine, many of these sauces can be served to vegans and people who are lactose intolerant.

# Green Onion Ginger

This deceptively simple sauce delivers flavor like nobody's business. It has such a high oil content that you can apply it sparingly and still be immersed in oniony, gingery goodness. Using freshly harvested scallions is key. If the tips have started to turn brown, they aren't fresh.

1 cup peanut oil

24 scallions, minced

1 cup minced fresh ginger

1 teaspoon salt

1. Heat the oil in a medium saucepan over medium heat. Add the scallions, ginger, and salt, and cook for 5 minutes, stirring often.

2. Cool the sauce in the refrigerator, then freeze according to the directions on page 2. The sauce will keep in the freezer for up to 6 months.

3. To serve, follow the directions on page 8 to reheat your sauce, then enjoy it on your choice of base at right.

# GREEN ONION GINGER MEALS TO MAKE

| BASE | QUANTITY | MEAL SUGGESTION |
|------|----------|-----------------|
| (page 12) | ¼ cup sauce per cup of cooked rice | Spoon sauce over rice. Garnish with chopped peanuts. Serve with sautéed bok choy. |
| (page 13) | ½ cup sauce per 14-ounce package of tofu | Toss pan-fried tofu with sauce. Serve with brown rice and green salad. |
| (page 14) | ½ cup sauce per pound of chicken | Spoon sauce over sliced chicken. Serve with white rice and sautéed Asian greens. |
| (page 15) | ½ cup sauce per pound of shrimp/ scallops | Toss sauce with pan-fried shrimp. Serve with sliced baguette and roasted zucchini. |
| (page 16) | ½ cup sauce per pound of fish | Spoon sauce over pan-fried fillets. Serve with sweet potatoes. |
| (page 17) | ½ cup sauce per pound of pork | Spoon sauce over sliced pork. Serve with mashed potatoes and sautéed mixed bell peppers. |
| (page 18) | ½ cup sauce per pound of beef | Spoon sauce over sliced beef. Serve with French fries and Caesar salad. |

## GREAT DIPPING SAUCE

My family's favorite way to use Green Onion Ginger is as a dipping sauce for a mixed plate of bite-size chicken chunks, steak bites, and scallops.

# Sambal

Sambal is a popular Asian sauce made with ground spices and chiles. There are variations across cultures; some use tomatoes or anchovies or even durian fruit! This version is a mainstream compilation.

1. Heat the oil in a large pan over medium heat. Add the shallots and salt, and sauté, stirring often, until the shallots are soft, about 7 minutes. Add the chiles and garlic, and cook, stirring, for 3 minutes longer.

2. Stir in the ginger, sugar, tamarind, chile powder, lemongrass, and turmeric, and reduce the heat to low. Sauté slowly until the mixture is fragrant, about 5 minutes.

3. Cool the sauce in the refrigerator, then freeze according to the directions on page 2. The sauce will keep in the freezer for up to 6 months.

4. To serve, heat the coconut milk in a small saucepan. Whisk in the thawed sambal, a tablespoon at a time, until the sauce reaches the desired spiciness. A touch of sambal is enough for some people, while others prefer more punch! Then enjoy the sauce on any one of the bases on the next page.

*At left:* Sliced pork with Sambal, bow tie pasta, and Caesar salad

5 tablespoons peanut oil

10 shallots or 5 medium onions, minced

Pinch of salt

8 chiles, any kind, minced

5 garlic cloves, minced or pressed

¼ cup minced fresh ginger

3 tablespoons sugar

2 tablespoons tamarind paste

1 tablespoon chile powder

1 tablespoon minced dried lemongrass

1 tablespoon ground turmeric

## FOR SERVING

1 (12-ounce) can coconut milk

# SAMBAL MEALS TO MAKE

| BASE | QUANTITY | MEAL SUGGESTION |
|------|----------|-----------------|
| *(page 12)* | ¼ cup sauce per cup of cooked rice | Spoon sauce over rice. Top with shredded coconut and chopped peanuts. Serve with green salad. |
| *(page 13)* | ½ cup sauce per 14-ounce package of tofu | Spoon sauce over pan-fried tofu. Serve with brown rice and sautéed spinach. |
| *(page 14)* | ½ cup sauce per pound of chicken | Spoon sauce over sliced chicken. Serve with sliced baguette and steamed broccoli. |
| *(page 15)* | ½ cup sauce per pound of shrimp/ scallops | Spoon sauce over pan-fried scallops. Serve with white rice and cabbage salad. |
| *(page 17)* | ½ cup sauce per pound of pork | *My Family's Favorite:* Spoon sauce over sliced pork. Serve with bow tie pasta and Caesar salad. |
| *(page 18)* | ½ cup sauce per pound of beef | Spoon sauce over sliced beef. Serve with hash browns and roasted eggplant. |

*Asian Inspired*

# Thai Peanut

In recent years, I've turned more and more frequently to cooking with nuts. They're a reliable source of protein and flavor, and they often give a dish just that little extra something it needs. Use this rich, nutty sauce to power through the last days of winter!

- 2 cups chicken or vegetable broth
- 1½ cups smooth peanut butter
- ¼ cup lime juice
- ¼ cup soy sauce
- 2 tablespoons sesame oil
- 2 red bell peppers, cored and thinly sliced
- ¼ cup minced fresh cilantro
- Red pepper flakes (optional)

**1.** Combine the broth, peanut butter, lime juice, soy sauce, and oil in a medium mixing bowl and whisk thoroughly. Add the bell peppers, cilantro, and pepper flakes to taste (if desired). Toss to combine.

**2.** Freeze according to the directions on page 2. The sauce will keep in the freezer for up to 6 months.

**3.** To serve, follow the directions on page 8 to heat your sauce, then enjoy it on any one of the bases on the next page. It's also good cold.

| BASE | QUANTITY | MEAL SUGGESTION |
|---|---|---|
| (page 10) | 1½ cups sauce per pound of pasta | *My Family's Favorite:* Spoon sauce over rice noodles. Garnish with shredded carrots, sliced red bell peppers, and chopped peanuts. Serve with mango salad. |
| (page 11) | ⅔ cup sauce per potato | Spoon sauce over potato. Top with bean sprouts and toasted coconut. Serve with green salad. |
| (page 12) | ½ cup sauce per cup of cooked rice | Spoon sauce over rice. Top with minced fresh cilantro and diced red bell pepper. |
| (page 13) | 1 cup sauce per 14-ounce package of tofu | Spoon sauce over pan-fried tofu. Serve with white rice and sliced papaya. |
| (page 14) | 1 cup sauce per pound of chicken | Spoon sauce over sliced chicken. Top with chopped peanuts. Serve with brown rice and steamed sliced carrots. |
| (page 15) | 1 cup sauce per pound of shrimp/scallops | Toss pan-fried shrimp with sauce. Serve with rice noodles and sautéed Asian greens. |
| (page 17) | 1 cup sauce per pound of pork | Spoon sauce over sliced pork. Top with chopped peanuts. Serve with soba noodles and roasted mixed bell peppers. |
| (page 18) | 1 cup sauce per pound of beef | Spoon sauce over sliced beef. Top with chopped peanuts. Serve with diced potatoes and spinach salad. |
| (page 21) | 3½ cups sauce, 1 cup coconut milk, and 1½ cups chicken broth per 4-serving pot | Top with chopped peanuts, diced red bell pepper, and crispy chow mein noodles. |

Rice noodles topped with
Thai Peanut sauce,
shredded carrots, sliced
bell peppers, and chopped
peanuts

65

# Spicy Soy

I like to reheat this sauce to a simmer and toss it to completely coat hot food before serving. It's so powerfully sweet, salty, *and* spicy that a thin coating is enough to flavor anything you want to put it on.

1 cup soy sauce

½ cup water

¼ cup seasoned rice vinegar

¼ cup minced fresh ginger

1 tablespoon honey

1 tablespoon Sriracha or other hot sauce

**1.** Combine the soy sauce, water, vinegar, ginger, honey, and hot sauce in a medium saucepan over medium heat. Cook for 5 minutes, stirring often.

**2.** Cool the sauce in the refrigerator, then freeze according to the directions on page 2. The sauce will keep in the freezer for up to 6 months.

**3.** To serve, follow the directions on page 8 to reheat your sauce, then enjoy it on your choice of base at right.

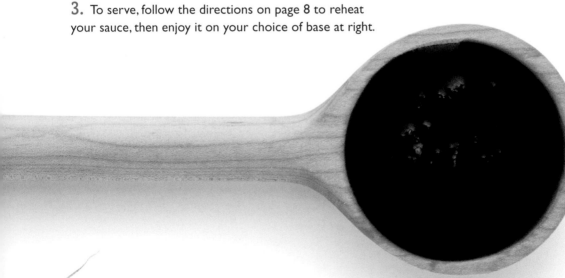

# SPICY SOY MEALS TO MAKE

| BASE | QUANTITY | MEAL SUGGESTION |
|---|---|---|
| (page 10) | ¾ cup sauce per pound of pasta | Spoon sauce over soba noodles. Toss with sliced hard-boiled egg. Serve with pan-fried eggplant. |
| (page 12) | ¼ cup sauce per cup of cooked rice | Spoon sauce over rice. Garnish with chopped peanuts. Serve with sautéed kale. |
| (page 13) | ½ cup sauce per 14-ounce package of tofu | *My Family's Favorite:* Toss pan-fried tofu with sauce. Serve with coconut rice and sliced mango. |
| (page 14) | ½ cup sauce per pound of chicken | Spoon sauce over sliced chicken. Serve with French fries and carrot sticks. |
| (page 15) | ½ cup sauce per pound of shrimp/ scallops | Toss pan-fried shrimp with sauce. Serve with ginger rice and sliced papaya. |
| (page 16) | ½ cup sauce per pound of fish | Spoon sauce over fillets. Serve with ramen noodles and steamed corn. |
| (page 17) | ½ cup sauce per pound of pork | Spoon sauce over sliced pork. Serve with baked sweet potatoes. |
| (page 18) | ½ cup sauce per pound of beef | Spoon sauce over sliced beef. Serve with mashed potatoes and sautéed Asian greens. |

# Spicy Shiitake

ABOUT 12 CUPS

Lauded for their medicinal properties in many traditions, shiitakes are one of my favorite mushrooms because they're just plain delicious. This hearty sauce uses Chinese spices and is best made with my Thai Peanut sauce (page 63). If you haven't made Thai Peanut sauce yet and are itching to try this recipe, a jarred peanut sauce will do.

8 cups chicken or mushroom broth

4 cups finely chopped dried shiitake mushrooms

2 cinnamon sticks

2 star anise pods

½ cup peanut sauce

4 medium onions, finely chopped

½ teaspoon salt

¼ cup minced fresh ginger

1 head garlic, cloves minced or pressed

2 chiles, seeded and minced

¼ cup soy sauce

1. Heat the broth in a large saucepan over low heat. Add the shiitakes, cinnamon sticks, and star anise pods. Cover and simmer until the mushrooms are soft, about 20 minutes.

2. In the meantime, combine the peanut sauce, onions, and salt in a large pot over medium heat. Sauté, stirring often, for 5 minutes. Add the ginger, garlic, and chiles, and cook for 3 minutes.

3. Remove the peanut sauce mixture from the heat and add the soy sauce. Stir to loosen any stuck-on bits on the bottom of the pan, and transfer the entire contents to the mushroom mixture. Simmer, covered, for 20 minutes. Remove and discard the cinnamon and star anise.

4. Cool the sauce in the refrigerator, then freeze according to the directions on page 2. The sauce will keep in the freezer for up to 6 months.

**5.** To serve, follow the directions on page 8 to reheat your sauce, then enjoy it on your choice of base below.

## SPICY SHIITAKE MEALS TO MAKE

| BASE | QUANTITY | MEAL SUGGESTION |
|---|---|---|
| (page 10) | 1½ cups sauce per pound of pasta | Spoon sauce over soba noodles. Serve with sautéed spinach. |
| (page 13) | 1 cup sauce per 14-ounce package of tofu | Spoon sauce over pan-fried tofu. Serve with white rice and sautéed Asian greens. |
| (page 14) | 1 cup sauce per pound of chicken | *My Family's Favorite:* Spoon sauce over sliced chicken. Serve with soba noodles and roasted Brussels sprouts. |
| (page 17) | 1 cup sauce per pound of pork | Spoon sauce over sliced pork. Serve with sliced baguette and tomato salad. |
| (page 18) | 1 cup sauce per pound of beef | Spoon sauce over sliced beef. Serve with mashed potatoes and steamed lima beans. |
| (page 20) | ¼ cup sauce per sandwich | Spread sauce evenly over horizontally sliced baguette. Top with sliced chicken and lettuce. |
| (page 21) | 3½ cups sauce and 2½ cups coconut milk per 4-serving pot | Garnish with crispy chow mein noodles. |

Pan-fried scallops
on a bed of Teriyaki
Spinach sauce and rice

# Teriyaki Spinach

Soy sauce, made from a fermented soy-bean paste, adds umami to this spinach sauce, while ginger and garlic round out the flavor. Use the best ginger you can find. If you can get your hands on ginger fresh enough to exude juice when you cut it, make lots of this!

4 tablespoons butter

4 medium to large onions, finely chopped

¼ cup soy sauce

¼ cup minced fresh ginger

1 head garlic, cloves minced or pressed

3 cups vegetable or chicken broth

22 ounces baby spinach (about 2 large tubs for most supermarket brands)

**1.** Warm the butter in a large stockpot over medium heat. Add the onions and soy sauce, and sauté, stirring frequently, until the onions are nearly soft, 5 to 8 minutes. Add the ginger and garlic, and sauté for 5 minutes longer.

**2.** Stir in the broth and spinach. Cover the pan and cook for 5 minutes. Remove the lid, stir, re-cover, and cook until the spinach is just cooked through, about 5 minutes longer.

**3.** Purée the mixture in the pan with an immersion blender, or transfer to a stand blender and purée.

**4.** Cool the sauce in the refrigerator, then freeze according to the directions on page 2. The sauce will keep in the freezer for up to 6 months.

**5.** To serve, follow the directions on page 8 to reheat your sauce, then enjoy it on any one of the bases on the next page.

| BASE | QUANTITY | MEAL SUGGESTION |
| --- | --- | --- |
| *(page 10)* | 2 cups sauce per pound of pasta | Spoon sauce over rigatoni. Top with crumbled bacon. |
| *(page 11)* | 1 cup sauce per potato | Spoon sauce over potato. Top with minced ham. |
| *(page 12)* | ¾ cup sauce per cup of cooked rice | Spoon sauce over rice. Top with crumbled bacon. |
| *(page 14)* | 1½ cups sauce per pound of chicken | Place sliced chicken on bed of sauce. Serve with udon noodles. |
| *(page 15)* | 1½ cups sauce per pound of shrimp/ scallops | *My Family's Favorite:* Place pan-fried scallops on bed of sauce. Serve with white rice. |
| *(page 16)* | 1½ cups sauce per pound of fish | Place pan-fried fillets on bed of sauce. Serve with baked potatoes. |
| *(page 17)* | 1½ cups sauce per pound of pork | Place sliced pork on bed of sauce. Serve with soba noodles. |
| *(page 18)* | 1½ cups sauce per pound of beef | Place sliced beef on bed of sauce. Serve with mashed potatoes. |
| *(page 20)* | ⅓ cup sauce per sandwich | Spread sauce evenly over sandwich bun. Top with sliced chicken and bean sprouts. |
| *(page 21)* | 4 cups sauce and 2 cups coconut milk per 4-serving pot | Garnish with bean sprouts. |

# Pineapple Ginger

The fresh-crushed pineapple makes all the difference in this mild yet highly flavorful sauce. In this case, canned won't do. Use the ripest, most fragrant pineapple you can find! The final sauce will coat anything you put it on with deliciousness — the more surface area, the better.

- 1 cup soy sauce
- 1 cup water
- ¼ cup cornstarch
- 1½ cups crushed fresh pineapple
- 1 cup honey
- 1 cup rice wine vinegar
- 4 garlic cloves, minced or pressed
- 2 tablespoons minced fresh ginger

1. Whisk the soy sauce, water, and cornstarch in stockpot over medium-high heat. Just as the mixture begins to boil, add the pineapple, honey, vinegar, garlic, and ginger. Reduce the heat to medium and continue to boil, whisking constantly, until the sauce begins to thicken. Remove from the heat.

2. Cool the sauce in the refrigerator, then freeze according to the directions on page 2. The sauce will keep in the freezer for up to 6 months.

3. To serve, follow the directions on page 8 to reheat your sauce, then enjoy it on any one of the bases on the next page.

# PINEAPPLE GINGER MEALS TO MAKE

| BASE | QUANTITY | MEAL SUGGESTION |
|------|----------|-----------------|
| *(page 12)* | ½ cup sauce per cup of cooked rice | Spoon sauce over rice. Top with chopped peanuts. Serve with baked winter squash. |
| *(page 14)* | I cup sauce per pound of chicken | *My Family's Favorite:* Spoon sauce over sliced chicken. Garnish with wedges of fresh pineapple. Serve with white rice and green salad. |
| *(page 15)* | I cup sauce per pound of shrimp/scallops | Toss pan-fried scallops with sauce. Serve with sliced baguette and baby carrots. |
| *(page 17)* | I cup sauce per pound of pork | Spoon sauce over sliced pork. Serve with boiled diced potatoes and tomato salad. |
| *(page 18)* | I cup sauce per pound of beef | Spoon sauce over sliced beef. Serve with soba noodles and sliced fresh pineapple. |

Asian Inspired

Sliced chicken with Pineapple Ginger sauce, rice, and green salad

# Hot Orange

Zesty notes of ginger and lime lie just beneath the orange in this lively concoction. Make it with only half the sambal if you don't want as much heat, or leave out the sambal altogether.

3 cups chicken or vegetable broth

¾ cup orange marmalade

¼ cup grated fresh ginger

¼ cup soy sauce

¼ cup lime juice

1 tablespoon homemade Sambal (page 61) or commercial sambal

1. Combine the broth, marmalade, ginger, and soy sauce in a medium saucepan over medium heat. Cook, stirring frequently, until the mixture boils and starts to thicken slightly, about 15 minutes. Remove from the heat, add the lime juice and sambal, and stir to combine.

2. Cool the sauce in the refrigerator, then freeze according to the directions on page 2. The sauce will keep in the freezer for up to 6 months.

3. To serve, follow the directions on page 8 to reheat your sauce, then enjoy it on your choice of base at right.

| BASE | QUANTITY | MEAL SUGGESTION |
|---|---|---|
|  (page 13) | ½ cup sauce per 14-ounce package of tofu | Toss pan-fried tofu with sauce. Top with chopped peanuts. Serve with soba noodles and green salad. |
| (page 14) | ½ cup sauce per pound of chicken | *My Family's Favorite:* Spoon sauce over sliced chicken. Serve with white rice and stir-fried green beans. |
| (page 15) | ½ cup sauce per pound of shrimp/ scallops | Toss pan-fried shrimp with sauce. Serve with vegetable fried rice. |
| (page 17) | ½ cup sauce per pound of pork | Spoon sauce over sliced pork. Serve with mashed potatoes and sautéed Asian greens. |
| (page 18) | ½ cup sauce per pound of beef | Spoon sauce over sliced beef. Serve with rice noodles and carrot salad. |
| (page 20) | 2 tablespoons sauce per sandwich | Spread sauce evenly over horizontally sliced baguette. Top with roast beef and shredded carrots. |

# Vietnamese Dipping Sauce

Serve this sauce in little bowls at the table so that each person may dip as little or as much as desired. If you love spicy food, habaneros are nice, but jalapeños work well, too. If you don't care for spicy food, leave out the chiles.

1½ cups warm water

½ cup firmly packed brown sugar

Juice and zest of 2 limes

4 garlic cloves, minced or pressed

2 chiles, minced (optional)

¼ cup fish sauce

1. Whisk together the water, sugar, and lime juice and zest in a medium mixing bowl. Add the garlic and chiles (if using), then stir in the fish sauce, 1 tablespoon at a time until you like the taste. Let rest for 10 minutes before freezing to allow the flavors to meld.

2. Freeze according to the directions on page 2. The sauce will keep in the freezer for up to 6 months.

3. To serve, follow the directions on page 8 to heat your sauce, then enjoy it with your choice of base at right.

# VIETNAMESE DIPPING SAUCE MEALS TO MAKE

| BASE | QUANTITY | MEAL SUGGESTION |
| --- | --- | --- |
| (page 14) | ½ cup sauce per pound of chicken | Spoon sauce over sliced chicken. Serve with white rice and steamed broccoli. |
| (page 13) | ½ cup sauce per 14-ounce package of tofu | Serve sauce in dipping cups with pan-fried tofu, brown rice, and green salad. |
| (page 15) | ½ cup sauce per pound of shrimp/scallops | Serve sauce in dipping cups with pan-fried shrimp, soba noodles, and stir-fried green beans. |
| (page 17) | ½ cup sauce per pound of pork | Spoon sauce over sliced pork. Serve with sliced baguette and pan-fried zucchini. |
| (page 18) | ½ cup sauce per pound of beef | Spoon sauce over sliced beef. Serve with rice noodles and mango salad. |

## MIX IT UP!

My family's favorite way to eat Vietnamese Dipping Sauce is with a mixed plate including pan-fried scallops, shrimp, and cubes of chicken.

# Coconut Lemon

I usually serve this unique, no-cook sauce on fish, but it is great on just about anything. If you don't like a lot of heat, try two chiles or just one. It's best with fresh lemon juice, but bottled will do in a pinch.

6 garlic cloves, minced or pressed

3 chiles, seeded and minced

3 tablespoons peanut oil

1 teaspoon salt

2 cups packed chopped fresh basil

3 (12-ounce) cans coconut milk

¾ cup lemon juice

1. Combine the garlic, chiles, oil, and salt in a blender and pulse three or four times. Add the basil and coconut milk, and blend until smooth. Add the lemon juice and blend again.

2. Freeze according to the directions on page 2. The sauce will keep in the freezer for up to 6 months.

3. To serve, follow the directions on page 8 to heat your sauce, then enjoy it on any one of the bases on page 82.

*At right:* Coconut Lemon sauce over pan-fried white fish, with gnocchi and sautéed green beans

*Asian Inspired*

# COCONUT LEMON MEALS TO MAKE

| BASE | QUANTITY | MEAL SUGGESTION |
|------|----------|-----------------|
| (page 10) | 1½ cups sauce per pound of pasta | Toss sauce with cavatappi. Serve with sautéed spinach. |
| (page 11) | ⅔ cup sauce per potato | Spoon sauce over potato. Serve with baked zucchini. |
| (page 12) | ½ cup sauce per cup of cooked rice | Toss sauce with rice. Garnish with basil flowers and serve with baked winter squash. |
| (page 13) | 1 cup sauce per 14-ounce package of tofu | Toss pan-fried tofu cubes with sauce. Serve with white rice and sautéed Asian greens. |
| (page 14) | 1 cup sauce per pound of chicken | Toss sauce with sliced chicken. Serve with biscuits and steamed lima beans. |
| (page 15) | 1 cup sauce per pound of shrimp/scallops | Toss sauce with pan-fried scallops. Serve with white rice and green salad. |
| (page 16) | 1 cup sauce per pound of fish | *My Family's Favorite:* Spoon sauce over pan-fried fillets. Serve with gnocchi and sautéed green beans. |
| (page 17) | 1 cup sauce per pound of pork | Spoon sauce over sliced pork. Serve with sliced baguette and sautéed kale. |
| (page 18) | 1 cup sauce per pound of beef | Spoon sauce over sliced beef. Serve with mashed potatoes and roasted bell peppers. |
| (page 20) | ¼ cup sauce per sandwich | Spread sauce evenly over horizontally sliced baguette. Top with sliced chicken and roasted bell peppers. |

# Curried Spinach

There are a lot of curry powders out there on the market. If you don't already have a favorite or two, it's worth trying a few to see what suits your taste. I prefer a medium-spicy Indian curry powder for this recipe.

6 tablespoons butter

4 medium to large onions, finely chopped

1 teaspoon salt

3 tablespoons curry powder

1 head garlic, cloves minced or pressed

3 cups vegetable or chicken broth

22 ounces baby spinach (about 2 large tubs for most supermarket brands)

1. Warm the butter in a large stockpot over medium heat. Add the onions and salt, and sauté, stirring frequently, until the onions are nearly soft, 5 to 8 minutes. Stir in the curry powder and garlic, and sauté for 5 minutes longer.

2. Add the broth and spinach. Cover the pan and cook for 5 minutes. Remove the lid, stir, re-cover, and cook until the spinach is just cooked through, another 2 to 3 minutes. Purée the mixture in the pan with an immersion blender, or transfer to a stand blender and purée.

3. Cool the curry in the refrigerator, then freeze according to the directions on page 2. The curry will keep in the freezer for up to 6 months.

4. To serve, follow the directions on page 8 to reheat your curry, then enjoy it on any one of the bases on page 85.

*Pan-fried steak on a bed of Curried Spinach sauce*

| BASE | QUANTITY | MEAL SUGGESTION |
|---|---|---|
| (page 10) | 2 cups curry per pound of pasta | Spoon curry over pasta. Garnish with chopped fresh basil. |
| (page 11) | 1 cup curry per potato | Spoon curry over potatoes. Serve with sliced mango. |
| (page 13) | 1½ cups curry per 14-ounce package of tofu | Place pan-fried tofu on bed of curry. Serve with white rice. |
| (page 14) | 1½ cups curry per pound of chicken | Place sliced chicken on bed of curry. Serve with coconut rice. |
| (page 15) | 1½ cups curry per pound of shrimp/scallops | Place pan-fried scallops on bed of curry. Serve with white rice. |
| (page 17) | 1½ cups curry per pound of pork | Place sliced pork on bed of curry. Serve with rice noodles. |
| (page 18) | 1½ cups curry per pound of beef | Place sliced beef on bed of curry. Serve with sliced baguette. |
| (page 20) | ⅓ cup curry per sandwich | Spread curry evenly over sliced baguette. Top with roasted chicken. |
| (page 21) | 4 cups curry and 2 cups coconut milk per 4-serving pot | *My Family's Favorite:* Serve with apple slices. |

# Yellow Curry

This is the mildest curry recipe in the book, for those who like the curry flavor without the heat. A favorite with kids, this sauce will please a wide audience!

2 tablespoons butter

1 large onion, finely chopped

¼ cup minced fresh ginger

1 head garlic, cloves minced or pressed

¼ cup yellow curry paste

¼ cup lime juice

3 (12-ounce) cans coconut milk

Salt and freshly ground black pepper

1. Warm the butter in a large pot over medium heat. Add the onion and ginger, and cook, stirring often, until the onion is cooked through, about 5 minutes.

2. Add the garlic, curry paste, and lime juice, and sauté, stirring, for 2 minutes. Add the coconut milk and salt and pepper to taste. Bring to a simmer and hold there for 2 minutes, then remove from the heat.

3. Cool the curry in the refrigerator, then freeze according to the directions on page 2. The curry will keep in the freezer for up to 6 months.

4. To serve, follow the directions on page 8 to reheat your curry, then enjoy it on any one of the bases on the next page.

**At left:** *Pan-fried tofu with Yellow Curry sauce, snow peas, and brown rice*

# YELLOW CURRY MEALS TO MAKE

| BASE | QUANTITY | MEAL SUGGESTION |
|---|---|---|
| (page 10) | 1½ cups curry per pound of pasta | Toss curry with rice noodles. Garnish with lime zest. Serve with sautéed Asian greens. |
| (page 12) | ½ cup curry per cup of cooked rice | Toss curry with rice. Top with chopped peanuts. Serve with baked winter squash. |
| (page 13) | 1 cup curry per 14-ounce package of tofu | *My Family's Favorite:* Toss curry with pan-fried tofu. Serve with brown rice and green or snow peas. |
| (page 14) | 1 cup curry per pound of chicken | Spoon curry over sliced chicken. Serve with white rice and green salad. |
| (page 15) | 1 cup curry per pound of shrimp/ scallops | Spoon curry over pan-fried scallops. Garnish with lime zest. Serve with sliced baguette and tomato salad. |
| (page 17) | 1 cup curry per pound of pork | Spoon curry over sliced pork. Serve with rice noodles and sliced mango. |
| (page 18) | 1 cup curry per pound of beef | Spoon curry over sliced beef. Serve with diced boiled potatoes and papaya salad. |

# Red Curry

MAKES
ABOUT 5 CUPS

Red curry is the baby bear of the three classic curries (yellow, green, and red). Not too hot and not too mild, it's the go-to curry in my kitchen to please a crowd. I love the earthy, umami notes of fish sauce, but not everyone cares for it. Feel free to leave it out if you prefer!

2 tablespoons peanut oil

3 bell peppers, all red or an assortment of colors, diced

1 large onion, diced

Pinch of salt

2 (12-ounce) cans coconut milk

¼ cup red curry paste

½ cup chopped bamboo shoots

⅓ cup minced fresh basil

2 tablespoons brown sugar

1–2 tablespoons fish sauce (optional)

1. Heat the oil in a large skillet over medium heat. Add the peppers, onion, and salt, and sauté, stirring often, until the peppers and onion are cooked through, 8 to 10 minutes. Remove from the heat and set aside.

2. Combine the coconut milk and curry paste in a medium saucepan and bring to a simmer over medium heat, whisking to mix. Cook for 5 minutes.

3. Stir in the pepper mixture, bamboo shoots, basil, sugar, and fish sauce (if using). Continue to simmer, stirring often, until the basil is limp but not overcooked, no more than 10 minutes.

4. Cool the curry in the refrigerator, then freeze according to the directions on page 2. The curry will keep in the freezer for up to 6 months.

5. To serve, follow the directions on page 8 to reheat your curry, then enjoy it on any one of the bases on the next page.

# RED CURRY MEALS TO MAKE

| BASE | QUANTITY | MEAL SUGGESTION |
|------|----------|-----------------|
| (page 10) | 1½ cups curry per pound of pasta | Toss curry with rice noodles. Garnish with basil flowers. |
| (page 11) | ¾ cup curry per potato | Spoon curry over potato. Serve with green salad. |
| (page 12) | ½ cup curry per cup of cooked rice | Spoon curry over rice. Serve with mango salad. |
| (page 13) | 1 cup curry per 14-ounce package of tofu | Spoon curry over pan-fried tofu. Serve with brown rice. |
| (page 14) | 1 cup curry per pound of chicken | Spoon curry over sliced chicken. Serve with coconut rice. |
| (page 15) | 1 cup curry per pound of shrimp/ scallops | *My Family's Favorite:* Toss pan-fried shrimp with curry. Serve with white rice. |
| (page 17) | 1 cup curry per pound of pork | Spoon curry over sliced pork. Serve with rice noodles. |
| (page 18) | 1 cup curry per pound of beef | Spoon curry over sliced beef. Serve with white rice. |

**At right:** *Pan-fried shrimp with Red Curry sauce and rice*

# Green Curry

MAKES

ABOUT 7 CUPS

This is the spiciest curry in the book. Use this recipe when you want to singe your tonsils! If you're not a fan of fish sauce, substitute soy sauce.

1. Heat the oil in a large saucepan over medium heat. Add the garlic and cook for 2 minutes. Add the coconut milk and curry paste, and cook, stirring, until the mixture comes to a simmer, 5 to 7 minutes. Stir in the green beans, fish sauce, sugar, and lime juice and zest. Simmer until the green beans are just cooked through but still firm, about 5 minutes. Remove from the heat and stir in the basil.

2. Cool the curry in the refrigerator, then freeze according to the directions on page 2. The curry will keep in the freezer for up to 6 months.

3. To serve, follow the directions on page 8 to reheat your curry, then enjoy it on your choice of base at right.

3 tablespoons peanut oil

4 garlic cloves, minced or pressed

3 (12-ounce) cans coconut milk

¼ cup green curry paste

3 cups bite-size green bean pieces

1 tablespoon fish sauce

1 tablespoon sugar

Juice and zest of 1 lime

1 cup finely chopped fresh basil

# GREEN CURRY MEALS TO MAKE

| BASE | QUANTITY | MEAL SUGGESTION |
|------|----------|-----------------|
| (page 12) | ½ cup curry per cup of cooked rice | Spoon curry over rice. Serve with mango salad. |
| (page 13) | I cup curry per 14-ounce package of tofu | Toss pan-fried tofu with curry. Serve with white rice. |
| (page 14) | I cup curry per pound of chicken | Spoon curry over sliced chicken. Serve with brown rice and sliced papaya. |
| (page 15) | I cup curry per pound of shrimp/scallops | *My Family's Favorite:* Toss pan-fried shrimp with curry. Serve with white rice. |
| (page 17) | I cup curry per pound of pork | Spoon curry over sliced pork. Serve with rice noodles. |
| (page 18) | I cup curry per pound of beef | Spoon curry over sliced beef. Serve with sliced baguette and papaya slices. |

**CHAPTER 3**

# MOSTLY MEDITERRANEAN

Some of my family's favorite flavor combinations come from those sunny countries around the Mediterranean Sea. The heat and sun of that region are perfect for growing basil, olives, tomatoes, lemon, and peppers — all of which practically beg to be whipped up into sauces!

# Vodka Cream Sauce

MAKES

ABOUT 10 CUPS

Vodka in a recipe serves several purposes at once: On a chemical level, it helps bind the acidic tomatoes to the cream without curdling it. On a taste level, it leaves a clean, sharp note after the alcohol cooks off.

4 tablespoons butter

2 medium onions, finely diced

1 teaspoon salt

4 garlic cloves, minced or pressed

2 teaspoons red pepper flakes

2 (28-ounce) cans diced tomatoes

1 cup vodka

1⅓ cups whipping cream

1 cup grated Parmesan cheese

1. Warm the butter in a large skillet over medium heat. Add the onions and salt, and sauté, stirring often, for 5 minutes. Add the garlic and pepper flakes, and cook, stirring, for 30 seconds longer.

2. Remove the pan from the heat and add the tomatoes and vodka. Stir to combine thoroughly, then return to the heat and cook, stirring often, until the alcohol evaporates, about 7 minutes.

3. Add the cream and Parmesan, and cook until the sauce thickens and the cheese is melted, about 5 minutes — but do not allow the sauce to boil.

4. Cool the sauce in the refrigerator, then freeze according to the directions on page 2. The sauce will keep in the freezer for up to 1 month.

5. To serve, follow the directions on page 8 to reheat your sauce, then enjoy it on any one of the bases on page 98.

*At right:* Meatball subs with Vodka Cream Sauce, mozzarella, and diced green peppers

# VODKA CREAM SAUCE MEALS TO MAKE

| BASE | QUANTITY | MEAL SUGGESTION |
|---|---|---|
| (page 10) | 1½ cups sauce per pound of pasta | Spoon sauce over linguine. Garnish with parsley. Serve with green salad. |
| (page 11) | ⅔ cup sauce per potato | Spoon sauce over potato. Serve with roasted turnips. |
| (page 14) | 1 cup sauce per pound of chicken | Spoon sauce over sliced chicken. Serve with white rice and steamed fiddleheads. |
| (page 15) | 1 cup sauce per pound of shrimp/ scallops | Spoon sauce over pan-fried scallops. Serve with sliced baguette and green bell pepper strips. |
| (page 17) | 1 cup sauce per pound of pork | Spoon sauce over sliced pork. Serve with wild rice blend and steamed green peas. |
| (page 18) | 1 cup sauce per pound of beef | Spoon sauce over sliced beef. Serve with French fries and spinach salad. |
| (page 20) | ¼ cup sauce per sandwich | *My Family's Favorite:* Toss sauce with meatballs and spread evenly over submarine roll. Top with sliced mozzarella cheese and diced green bell pepper. |

# Primavera

You want to shop at your farmers' market for the ingredients in this sauce if you can! A good primavera depends upon freshly harvested, tender young vegetables. If you have some cherry tomatoes at hand, slice them in half and toss them on top of the sauce when you serve it.

12 young carrots, diced

12 young summer squash (no larger than a hot dog), diced

8 young onions, diced

2 cups diced red bell pepper

½ cup extra-virgin olive oil

Salt and freshly ground black pepper

2 cups white wine

1 cup finely chopped fresh basil

1. Preheat the oven to 400°F/200°C.

2. Combine the carrots, squash, onions, and bell peppers in a large baking dish, drizzle with the oil, season with salt and black pepper to taste, and toss to mix. Roast the vegetables for 15 minutes, then transfer the dish to a heatproof surface.

3. Immediately add the wine to the hot pan and stir to combine. Let the sauce cool for 10 minutes, then stir in the basil.

4. Cool the sauce in the refrigerator, then freeze according to the directions on page 2. The sauce will keep in the freezer for up to 6 months.

5. To serve, follow the directions on page 8 to reheat your sauce, then enjoy it on any one of the bases on page 101.

| BASE | QUANTITY | MEAL SUGGESTION |
|---|---|---|
| (page 10) | 2 cups sauce per pound of pasta | Spoon sauce over cavatappi. Garnish with grated Parmesan cheese. |
| (page 11) | 1 cup sauce per potato | Spoon sauce over potato. Top with grated Parmesan cheese. |
| (page 12) | ¾ cup sauce per cup of cooked rice | Spoon sauce over rice. Top with shredded mozzarella cheese. |
| (page 14) | 1½ cups sauce per pound of chicken | Spoon sauce over chicken slices. Serve with mashed potatoes. |
| (page 15) | 1½ cups sauce per pound of shrimp/ scallops | Toss pan-fried shrimp with sauce. Serve with white rice. |
| (page 16) | 1½ cups sauce per pound of fish | Spoon sauce over pan-fried fillets. Serve with brown rice. |
| (page 17) | 1½ cups sauce per pound of pork | Spoon sauce over sliced pork. Serve with sliced baguette. |
| (page 18) | 1½ cups sauce per pound of beef | Spoon sauce over sliced beef. Serve with hash browns. |
| (page 21) | 4 cups sauce and 2 cups half-and-half or broth per 4-serving pot | *My Family's Favorite:* Garnish with chopped parsley and croutons. |

**At left:** *Primavera soup with croutons and chopped parsley*

# Parmesan Leek

MAKES

---

ABOUT 8 CUPS

The leek is an overgrown, underrated cousin to onion and garlic. Its subtle but immersive flavor easily makes a meal out of any carbohydrate base. Heck, I'd have it with toast and call it dinner!

¾ cup (1½ sticks) butter

4 leeks, white and pale green parts only, rinsed and finely chopped

8 garlic cloves, minced or pressed

1 teaspoon salt

½ cup all-purpose flour

4 cups milk

1 cup grated Parmesan cheese

1 cup small walnut pieces

4 strips bacon, cooked and crumbled (optional)

1. Warm the butter in a large skillet over medium heat. Add the leeks, garlic, and salt, and sauté, stirring often, until the leeks are limp and cooked through, 5 to 7 minutes. Stir in the flour and cook, stirring, for 2 minutes longer.

2. Whisk in the milk and continue whisking until the sauce begins to thicken, about 5 minutes. Add the Parmesan, walnuts, and bacon (if using), and cook, stirring, for 3 minutes.

3. Cool the sauce in the refrigerator, then freeze according to the directions on page 2. The sauce will keep in the freezer for up to 1 month.

4. To serve, follow the directions on page 8 to reheat your sauce, then enjoy it on your choice of base at right.

# PARMESAN LEEK MEALS TO MAKE

| BASE | QUANTITY | MEAL SUGGESTION |
|---|---|---|
| (page 10) | 1½ cups sauce per pound of pasta | Spoon sauce over fettucine. Garnish with parsley. Serve with green salad. |
| (page 11) | ⅔ cup sauce per potato | *My Family's Favorite:* Spoon sauce over potato. Serve with succotash. |
| (page 12) | ½ cup sauce per cup of cooked rice | Spoon sauce over rice. Garnish with parsley and additional crumbled bacon. Serve with stir-fried pea pods. |
| (page 14) | 1 cup sauce per pound of chicken | Spoon sauce over sliced chicken. Serve with Italian bread slices and tomato salad. |
| (page 15) | 1 cup sauce per pound of shrimp/ scallops | Spoon sauce over pan-fried scallops. Serve with white rice and steamed asparagus. |
| (page 21) | 3½ cups sauce and 2½ cups vegetable or chicken broth per 4-serving pot | Garnish with minced parsley. Serve with crackers. |

# Arrabiata

This is a warm-your-blood fall and winter recipe. Both oregano and rosemary do well in cooler weather, so after summer's basil is long gone, these two will be the stars in your garden or at your farmers' market.

1. Heat the oil in a large saucepan over medium heat. Add the onions and salt, and sauté, stirring often, until the onions are soft, 6 to 8 minutes. Stir in the tomatoes, tomato paste, olives, corn, garlic, oregano, rosemary, and pepper flakes, and cook, stirring frequently, for 5 minutes longer.

2. Cool the sauce in the refrigerator, then freeze according to the directions on page 2. The sauce will keep in the freezer for up to 6 months.

3. To serve, follow the directions on page 8 to reheat your sauce, then enjoy it on your choice of base at right.

- ½ cup extra-virgin olive oil
- 4 onions, finely diced
- ½ teaspoon salt
- 2 (28-ounce) cans diced tomatoes
- 1 cup tomato paste
- 1 cup pitted diced black olives
- 1 cup corn kernels, fresh or frozen
- 1 head garlic, cloves minced or pressed
- 2 tablespoons minced fresh oregano
- 2 tablespoons minced fresh rosemary
- 2 tablespoons red pepper flakes

# ARRABIATA MEALS TO MAKE

| BASE | QUANTITY | MEAL SUGGESTION |
|------|----------|-----------------|
| (page 10) | 2 cups sauce per pound of pasta | *My Family's Favorite:* Spoon sauce over spaghetti. Top with grated Romano cheese. Serve with green salad. |
| (page 11) | 1 cup sauce per potato | Spoon sauce over potato. Top with grated Romano cheese. Serve with roasted asparagus. |
| (page 14) | 1 cup sauce per pound of chicken | Spoon sauce over sliced chicken. Serve with scalloped potatoes and steamed pea pods. |
| (page 17) | 1 cup sauce per pound of pork | Spoon sauce over sliced pork. Serve with potato wedges and roasted mixed bell peppers. |
| (page 18) | 1 cup sauce per pound of beef | Spoon sauce over sliced beef. Serve with white rice and roasted carrots. |
| (page 20) | ⅓ cup sauce per sandwich | Spread sauce evenly over sandwich bun. Top with sliced turkey and mozzarella cheese. |

# Eggplant Ragu

First domesticated in Asia, eggplant has been popular all over the world for centuries. It's one of the best vegetables to substitute for meat to bring substance and texture to a sauce, as in this hearty ragu.

1. Heat the oil in a large pot over medium heat. Add the eggplant, onions, bell peppers, celery, and salt, and cook, stirring often, until the vegetables are very soft, about 15 minutes.

2. Add the garlic, thyme, and rosemary, and cook, stirring, for 2 minutes. Stir in the tomatoes, tomato paste, and water. Reduce the heat to low and cook, stirring often, for 30 minutes. Add black pepper to taste.

3. Cool the sauce in the refrigerator, then freeze according to the directions on page 2. The sauce will keep in the freezer for up to 6 months.

4. To serve, follow the directions on page 8 to reheat your sauce, then enjoy it on your choice of base at right.

¼ cup extra-virgin olive oil

1 large or 2 small eggplant, diced

2 medium onions, finely chopped

2 green bell peppers, finely chopped

2 red bell peppers, finely chopped

3 celery stalks, finely chopped

1 teaspoon salt

6 garlic cloves, minced or pressed

¼ cup minced fresh thyme

3 tablespoons minced fresh rosemary

2 (28-ounce) cans chopped tomatoes

1 cup tomato paste

3 cups water

Freshly ground black pepper

# EGGPLANT RAGU MEALS TO MAKE

| BASE | QUANTITY | MEAL SUGGESTION |
|---|---|---|
| (page 10) | 2 cups sauce per pound of pasta | Spoon sauce over fettucine. Top with grated Parmesan cheese. |
| (page 11) | 1 cup sauce per potato | *My Family's Favorite:* Spoon sauce over potato. Top with grated Parmesan cheese. |
| (page 14) | 1 cup sauce per pound of chicken | Spoon sauce over sliced chicken. Serve with white rice. |
| (page 20) | 1/3 cup sauce per sandwich | Spread sauce evenly over horizontally sliced baguette. Top with sliced mozzarella cheese. |
| (page 21) | 4 cups sauce and 2 cups vegetable or chicken broth per 4-serving pot | Garnish with grated Parmesan cheese. |

# Balsamic Onion

While it's always true that high-quality ingredients are key to a high-quality finished product, it's especially true for balsamic vinegar. Choose one you love!

- 4 medium onions, very thinly sliced
- ⅔ cup extra-virgin olive oil
- ⅔ cup balsamic vinegar
- 2 tablespoons minced fresh oregano
- 2 teaspoons salt
- 2 teaspoons freshly ground black pepper
- 2 cups chicken broth

1. Preheat the oven to 375°F/190°C. Lightly oil a rimmed baking sheet.

2. Combine the onions, oil, half of the vinegar, oregano, salt, and pepper in a large mixing bowl. Toss thoroughly. Place on the oiled baking sheet and bake for about 30 minutes, until the onions are soft and cooked through.

3. Toss the hot onions with the remaining vinegar. Combine the onion mixture with the broth in a medium saucepan over medium-low heat. Bring to a simmer and cook, stirring often, for 10 minutes.

4. Cool the sauce in the refrigerator, then freeze according to the directions on page 2. The sauce will keep in the freezer for up to 6 months.

5. To serve, follow the directions on page 8 to reheat your sauce, then enjoy it on your choice of base at right.

# BALSAMIC ONION MEALS TO MAKE

| BASE | QUANTITY | MEAL SUGGESTION |
|------|----------|-----------------|
| *(page 14)* | 1 cup sauce per pound of chicken | Spoon sauce over sliced chicken. Serve with sliced baguette and pan-fried mushrooms. |
| *(page 17)* | 1 cup sauce per pound of pork | *My Family's Favorite:* Spoon sauce over sliced pork. Serve with mashed potatoes and steamed green peas. |
| *(page 18)* | 1 cup sauce per pound of beef | Spoon sauce over sliced beef. Serve with white rice and green salad. |

*Sliced pork with Roasted Red Pepper sauce, hash browns, and green peas*

# Roasted Red Pepper

If you've never roasted peppers before, don't be afraid to give it a try. The roasting process brings out a depth of flavor you can't get any other way.

1. Position an oven rack just below the broiler. Preheat the broiler. Line a baking sheet with parchment paper.

2. Toss the bell peppers with 1 tablespoon of the oil in a large mixing bowl. Arrange the strips, skin side up, on the prepared baking sheet, making sure that the strips are flat enough to avoid direct contact with the broiler element. Do not overlap strips.

3. Broil the bell peppers until the skins are charred and the flesh is limp, 10 to 15 minutes, depending on the thickness of the peppers. Remove from the oven and set aside to cool.

4. In the meantime, heat the remaining oil in a stockpot over medium heat. Add the jalapeños, onions, and salt, and sauté, stirring often, until the onion is soft, about 5 minutes. Add the garlic and cook for 2 minutes longer. Stir in the broth and black pepper to taste, and reduce the heat to low.

5. Once the broiled peppers are cool enough, remove the charred skins by hand and discard. Chop the flesh into small pieces and add to the broth mixture. Simmer for 20 minutes, then purée in the pan with an immersion blender, or transfer to a stand blender and purée. Add additional black pepper, if desired.

10 red bell peppers, seeded and cut into large strips

⅓ cup extra-virgin olive oil

3 jalapeños, seeded and minced

2 medium onions, finely chopped

½ teaspoon salt

1 head garlic, cloves minced or pressed

5 cups chicken or vegetable broth

Freshly ground black pepper

*Recipe continues on the next page*

**6.** Cool the sauce in the refrigerator, then freeze according to the directions on page 2. The sauce will keep in the freezer for up to 6 months.

**7.** To serve, follow the directions on page 8 to reheat your sauce, then enjoy it on your choice of base below.

## ROASTED RED PEPPER MEALS TO MAKE

| BASE | QUANTITY | MEAL SUGGESTION |
|---|---|---|
| *(page 10)* | 1½ cups sauce per pound of pasta | Spoon sauce over gemelli. Top with grated Parmesan cheese. Serve with green salad. |
| *(page 11)* | ⅔ cup sauce per potato | Spoon sauce over potato. Top with grated cheddar cheese. Serve with baby carrots. |
| *(page 14)* | 1 cup sauce per pound of chicken | Spoon sauce over sliced chicken. Serve with bow tie pasta and steamed broccoli. |
| *(page 15)* | 1 cup sauce per pound of shrimp/ scallops | Place pan-fried scallops on bed of sauce. Serve with white rice and sautéed kale. |
| *(page 16)* | 1 cup sauce per pound of fish | Spoon sauce over pan-fried fillets. Serve with sliced baguette and roasted beets. |
| *(page 17)* | 1 cup sauce per pound of pork | *My Family's Favorite:* Spoon sauce over sliced pork. Serve with hash browns and steamed green peas. |
| *(page 18)* | 1 cup sauce per pound of beef | Spoon sauce over sliced beef. Serve with couscous and roasted cauliflower. |
| *(page 21)* | 3½ cups sauce and 2½ cups vegetable or chicken broth per 4-serving pot | Top with a dollop of sour cream and croutons. |

# Herbed Dijonnaise

MAKES

ABOUT 1½ CUPS

Piquant and fresh-tasting, this no-cook sauce will enliven the senses and warm the blood. Think of it as a reset button for a difficult day straight from Dijon, France, to your kitchen! In fact, you can keep a little of this sauce in the fridge for salads or steamed veggies, too — it'll perk up just about anything.

¾ cup Dijon mustard

⅓ cup white wine

¼ cup extra-virgin olive oil

1 tablespoon minced fresh basil

1 tablespoon minced fresh rosemary

1 teaspoon minced fresh oregano

1 teaspoon minced fresh thyme

Freshly ground black pepper

1. Combine the mustard, wine, oil, basil, rosemary, oregano, thyme, and pepper to taste in a medium mixing bowl and whisk until thoroughly blended. Let rest for 10 minutes to allow the flavors to meld.

2. Freeze according to the directions on page 2. The sauce will keep in the freezer for up to 6 months (or in the refrigerator for 2 weeks).

3. To serve, follow the directions on page 8 to heat your sauce, then enjoy it on any one of the bases on the next page.

# HERBED DIJONNAISE MEALS TO MAKE

| BASE | QUANTITY | MEAL SUGGESTION |
|------|----------|-----------------|
| (page 14) | ½ cup sauce per pound of chicken | Spoon sauce over sliced chicken. Serve with French fries and roasted asparagus. |
| (page 17) | ½ cup sauce per pound of pork | *My Family's Favorite:* Drizzle over sliced pork. Serve with sliced baguette and roasted cauliflower. |
| (page 18) | ½ cup sauce per pound of beef | Spoon sauce over sliced beef. Serve with white rice and green salad. |
| (page 20) | 2 tablespoons sauce per sandwich | Spread sauce evenly over bread. Top with ham and sliced Emmental cheese. |

*At right:* *Herbed Dijonnaise sauce over sliced chicken, with French fries and roasted asparagus*

# Lemon Egg

Known as *avgolemono* in Greece, this classic sauce is popular throughout the Mediterranean. In addition to the dinner options below, try Lemon Egg sauce as a dip for steamed artichokes for parties.

8 large eggs, separated

½ cup lemon juice

1 tablespoon all-purpose flour

1 teaspoon salt

4 cups chicken or vegetable broth

Salt and freshly ground black pepper

1. Combine the eggs yolks, lemon juice, and flour in a medium mixing bowl. Whisk until thoroughly combined, about 2 minutes.

2. Beat the egg whites and salt in a second medium mixing bowl with an electric beater until they are light and fluffy, about 5 minutes. Slowly add the egg yolk mixture to the beaten whites, whisking constantly.

3. Fill the bottom of a double boiler with about 1 inch of water and place over medium heat. Pour the broth into the top of the double boiler and heat to a simmer, then slowly add the egg mixture, whisking constantly. Cook, whisking, until the sauce just begins to thicken, about 2 minutes. Remove from the heat and season with salt and pepper to taste.

4. Cool the sauce in the refrigerator, then freeze according to the directions on page 2. The sauce will keep in the freezer for up to 6 months.

5. To serve, follow the directions on page 8 to reheat your sauce, then enjoy it on your choice of base at right.

| BASE | QUANTITY | MEAL SUGGESTION |
|---|---|---|
| (page 10) | 1½ cups sauce per pound of pasta | Spoon sauce over gemelli. Season liberally with pepper. Serve with green salad. |
| (page 11) | ⅔ cup sauce per potato | Spoon sauce over potato. Serve with roasted mixed bell peppers. |
| (page 12) | ½ cup sauce per cup of cooked rice | Spoon sauce over rice. Serve with baked winter squash. |
| (page 14) | 1 cup sauce per pound of chicken | Spoon sauce over sliced chicken. Serve with sliced baguette and steamed green beans. |
| (page 15) | 1 cup sauce per pound of shrimp/scallops | Spoon sauce over pan-fried shrimp. Serve with white rice and Greek salad. |
| (page 16) | 1 cup sauce per pound of fish | Spoon sauce over pan-fried fillets. Serve with brown rice and steamed zucchini. |
| (page 17) | 1 cup sauce per pound of pork | Spoon sauce over sliced pork. Serve with pita bread and fresh cucumbers. |
| (page 18) | 1 cup sauce per pound of beef | Spoon sauce over sliced beef. Serve with new potatoes and pan-fried sliced turnips. |
| (page 21) | 3½ cups sauce and 2½ cups chicken or vegetable broth per 4-serving pot | *My Family's Favorite:* **Add** finely diced chicken. Garnish with chopped parsley. |

# Mustard Greens Anchovy

MAKES

ABOUT 6 CUPS

Mustard greens are one of my favorite garden-to-kitchen plants. They are easy to cultivate, so planting a few mustard greens is a much faster and more convenient way to grow my own spicy food than nurturing slow and temperamental hot peppers. Plus, they're a green vegetable. Talk about a win-win!

2 pounds mustard greens, stems removed, leaves roughly chopped (12 cups raw)

10 anchovies, finely diced

3 cups mushroom broth

½ cup extra-virgin olive oil

Zest and juice of 2 lemons

1–2 teaspoons red pepper flakes

1. Combine the mustard greens, anchovies, broth, oil, lemon zest and juice, and pepper flakes in a large stockpot. Cover and bring to a simmer over medium heat. Cook, stirring occasionally, until the greens are cooked through, about 12 minutes.

2. Purée the mixture in the pan with an immersion blender, or transfer to a stand blender and purée.

3. Cool the sauce in the refrigerator, then freeze according to the directions on page 2. The sauce will keep in the freezer for up to 6 months.

4. To serve, follow the directions on page 8 to reheat your sauce, then enjoy it on your choice of base at right.

Mostly Mediterranean

# MUSTARD GREENS ANCHOVY MEALS TO MAKE

| BASE | QUANTITY | MEAL SUGGESTION |
|------|----------|-----------------|
| (page 10) | 2 cups sauce per pound of pasta | Spoon sauce over penne. Top with grated Romano cheese. |
| (page 11) | 1 cup sauce per potato | Spoon sauce over potato. Top with grated Romano cheese. |
| (page 12) | ¾ cup sauce per cup of cooked rice | Spoon sauce over rice. Top with grated Romano cheese. |
| (page 14) | 1½ cups sauce per pound of chicken | Arrange sliced chicken on bed of sauce. Serve with white rice. |
| (page 15) | 1½ cups sauce per pound of shrimp/scallops | *My Family's Favorite:* Arrange pan-fried scallops on bed of sauce. Serve with wild rice and steamed winter squash. |
| (page 17) | 1½ cups sauce per pound of pork | Arrange sliced pork on bed of sauce. Serve with mashed potatoes. |
| (page 18) | 1½ cups sauce per pound of beef | Arrange sliced beef on bed of sauce. Serve with sliced baguette. |
| (page 20) | ⅓ cup sauce per sandwich | Spread sauce evenly over sandwich bun. Top with sliced Havarti cheese. |

# Anchovy Dill

MAKES
---
ABOUT 6 CUPS

Oily, brined anchovies pack a wallop of flavor in any dish. In this sauce, they combine with fresh dill, parsley, and basil to flood your palate with summery goodness, especially when it's served with fruit. The tang of lemon breaks through just like sunshine!

1. Combine the olives, Parmesan, oil, parsley, basil, dill, lemon juice and zest, anchovies, garlic, and pepper in a large mixing bowl and mix well. Let sit for 5 minutes to allow the flavors to meld before freezing.

2. Freeze according to the directions on page 2. The sauce will keep in the freezer for up to 6 months.

3. To serve, follow the directions on page 8 to heat your sauce, then enjoy it on your choice of base at right.

- 2 cups pitted and finely chopped green olives
- 1 cup grated Parmesan cheese
- 1 cup extra-virgin olive oil
- 1½ cups minced fresh parsley
- 1 cup finely chopped fresh basil
- ¼ cup minced fresh dill
- Juice and zest of 2 lemons
- 8 anchovies, minced
- 2 garlic cloves, minced or pressed
- 1 teaspoon freshly ground black pepper

# ANCHOVY DILL MEALS TO MAKE

| BASE | QUANTITY | MEAL SUGGESTION |
|---|---|---|
| (page 10) | 1½ cups sauce per pound of pasta | Spoon sauce over cavatappi. Serve with sliced apples. |
| (page 12) | ½ cup sauce per cup of cooked rice | Spoon sauce over rice. Serve with sliced pears. |
| (page 14) | 1 cup sauce per pound of chicken | Spoon sauce over sliced chicken. Serve with pita and cantaloupe. |
| (page 15) | 1 cup sauce per pound of shrimp/ scallops | Spoon sauce over pan-fried scallops. Serve with focaccia and honeydew melon. |
| (page 16) | 1 cup sauce per pound of fish | *My Family's Favorite:* Spoon sauce over pan-fried fillets. Serve with pasta salad and grapes. |
| (page 17) | 1 cup sauce per pound of pork | Spoon sauce over sliced pork. Serve with sliced baguette and cherries. |
| (page 18) | 1 cup sauce per pound of beef | Spoon sauce over sliced beef. Serve with toasted bagels and bananas. |

# Sage Pancetta Mushroom

MAKES

ABOUT 5 CUPS

Pancetta is similar to bacon, but it's cured, not smoked, which gives it a different flavor. Although it should be cooked for this recipe, pancetta is often eaten raw in Italy (if you have a bit left over, give it a try and see what you think!). Both the pancetta and the mushrooms in this sauce produce earthy notes, while sage balances the flavor.

½ cup (1 stick) butter

5 cups minced mushrooms, any variety

1½ cups finely diced pancetta

2 tablespoons crumbled dried sage

Freshly ground black pepper

½ cup white wine

½ cup half-and-half

1. Warm the butter in a large skillet over medium-high heat. Add the mushrooms, pancetta, sage, and a generous amount of pepper. Cook, stirring frequently, until any excess moisture steams off, the butter browns, and the mushrooms are cooked through, 8 to 10 minutes.

2. Add the wine and half-and-half to the mushroom mixture. Stir until completely mixed, then remove from the heat.

3. Cool the sauce in the refrigerator, then freeze according to the directions on page 2. The sauce will keep in the freezer for up to 6 months.

4. To serve, follow the directions on page 8 to reheat your sauce, then enjoy it on your choice of base at right.

## SAGE PANCETTA MUSHROOM MEALS TO MAKE

| BASE | QUANTITY | MEAL SUGGESTION |
|---|---|---|
| (page 10) | ¾ cup sauce per pound of pasta | *My Family's Favorite:* Spoon sauce over spaghetti. Top with grated Romano cheese. Serve with steamed green peas. |
| (page 11) | ⅓ cup sauce per potato | Spoon sauce over potato. Top with grated Romano cheese. Serve with green salad. |
| (page 12) | ¼ cup sauce per cup of cooked rice | Spoon sauce over rice. Top with grated Romano cheese. Serve with baked winter squash. |
| (page 14) | ½ cup sauce per pound of chicken | Spoon sauce over sliced chicken. Serve with wild rice and baby carrots. |
| (page 15) | ½ cup sauce per pound of shrimp | Place pan-fried shrimp on bed of sauce. Serve with white rice and sautéed spinach. |
| (page 20) | 2 tablespoons sauce per sandwich | Spread sauce evenly over horizontally sliced baguette. Top with sliced mozzarella cheese. |

# Meyer Lemon Spinach

MAKES
———
ABOUT 8 CUPS

You can make this recipe with a regular lemon, but I love it with the sweeter taste of the Meyer lemon, which is a hybrid of a regular lemon and a mandarin orange.

¾ cup extra-virgin olive oil

6 garlic cloves, minced or pressed

3 (10-ounce) packages frozen chopped spinach

1 tablespoon red pepper flakes

Juice and zest of 3 Meyer lemons

Freshly ground black pepper

2 cups plain whole-milk yogurt

1. Heat the oil in a large stockpot over medium heat. Add the garlic and cook, stirring, for 1 minute. Add the spinach and pepper flakes, and cook until the spinach is warm, about 10 minutes.

2. Add the lemon juice and zest and black pepper to taste. Stir thoroughly, and cook for 2 minutes longer. Remove from the heat, add the yogurt, and stir.

3. Cool the sauce in the refrigerator, then freeze according to the directions on page 2. The sauce will keep in the freezer for up to 2 months.

4. To serve, follow the directions on page 8 to reheat your sauce, then enjoy it on any one of the bases on the next page.

*At left: Pan-fried scallops on a bed of Meyer Lemon Spinach sauce and rice*

# MEYER LEMON SPINACH MEALS TO MAKE

| BASE | QUANTITY | MEAL SUGGESTION |
|------|----------|-----------------|
| (page 10) | 1½ cups sauce per pound of pasta | Spoon sauce over rigatoni. Serve with green salad. |
| (page 11) | ⅔ cup sauce per potato | Spoon sauce over potato. Top with grated Parmesan cheese. |
| (page 12) | ½ cup sauce per cup of cooked rice | Spoon sauce over rice. Top with grated Parmesan cheese. |
| (page 14) | 1 cup sauce per pound of chicken | Arrange sliced chicken on bed of sauce. Serve with sliced baguette. |
| (page 15) | 1 cup sauce per pound of shrimp/scallops | *My Family's Favorite:* Arrange pan-fried scallops on bed of sauce. Serve with brown rice. |
| (page 16) | 1 cup sauce per pound of fish | Arrange fish fillets on bed of sauce. Serve with white rice. |
| (page 17) | 1 cup sauce per pound of pork | Arrange pork slices on bed of sauce. Serve with mashed potatoes. |
| (page 18) | 1 cup sauce per pound of beef | Arrange beef slices on bed of sauce. Serve with gnocchi. |
| (page 20) | ¼ cup sauce per sandwich | Spread sauce evenly over sandwich bun. Top with sliced Swiss cheese. |
| (page 21) | 3½ cups sauce and 2½ cups broth per 4-serving pot | Serve with biscuits. |

# Sausage Ragu

This is one of my trickiest trickster sauces for getting both veggies and protein into tired, cranky people. Break out a batch of this and a loaf of bread to get the most nutritious meal with the least amount of work!

6 tablespoons extra-virgin olive oil

1½ pounds loose Italian sausage

2 medium onions, finely chopped

2 green bell peppers, finely chopped

2 red bell peppers, finely chopped

3 celery stalks, finely chopped

6 garlic cloves, minced or pressed

¼ cup minced fresh thyme

3 tablespoons minced fresh rosemary

2 (28-ounce) cans chopped tomatoes

1 cup tomato paste

3 cups water

Freshly ground black pepper

1. Heat the oil in a large skillet over medium heat. Add the sausage and cook, breaking up the meat and stirring often, until completely browned, about 10 minutes. Remove the sausage with a slotted spoon and transfer to a paper towel–lined plate to drain.

2. Drain off most of the oil from the hot pan, then return the pan to the stove, reduce the heat to low, and add the onions, bell peppers, and celery. Cook, stirring often, until the vegetables are very soft, about 12 minutes.

3. Add the garlic, thyme, and rosemary, and cook, stirring, for 2 minutes. Stir in the tomatoes, tomato paste, and water. Cook over low heat, stirring often, for 30 minutes. Add the sausage and black pepper to taste.

4. Cool the sauce in the refrigerator, then freeze according to the directions on page 2. The sauce will keep in the freezer for up to 6 months.

5. To serve, follow the directions on page 8 to reheat your sauce, then enjoy it on any one of the bases on the next page. You may want to add a bit of cream and/or Parmesan cheese to the sauce when you reheat it.

# SAUSAGE RAGU MEALS TO MAKE

| BASE | QUANTITY | MEAL SUGGESTION |
|---|---|---|
| (page 10) | 2 cups sauce per pound of pasta | *My Family's Favorite:* Spoon sauce over fettuccine. Top with grated Parmesan cheese and freshly ground black pepper. Serve with green salad. |
| (page 11) | 1 cup sauce per potato | Spoon sauce over potato. Top with ¼ cup shredded cheddar cheese. |
| (page 20) | ⅓ cup sauce per sandwich | Spread sauce evenly over horizontally sliced baguette. Top with sliced Monterey Jack cheese. |
| (page 21) | 4 cups sauce and 2 cups half-and-half per 4-serving pot | Serve with biscuits. |

**At right:** *Fettucine with Sausage Ragu sauce*

# Harissa

MAKES

ABOUT 2 CUPS

A little of this Tunisian sauce goes a long way. Harissa is traditionally used as a flavoring for couscous, fish stew, chicken, goat, or lamb. You can also stir it into any stew or soup, or combine a bit with olive oil and use it as a dip or spread for bread.

6 red bell peppers, finely chopped

2 chiles

1 cup extra-virgin olive oil

2 tablespoons whole coriander seed

2 tablespoons whole caraway seed

8 garlic cloves, minced or pressed

2 tablespoons sugar

Salt and freshly ground black pepper

1. Position an oven rack just below the broiler. Preheat the broiler. Toss the bell peppers and and chiles with ½ cup of the oil on a rimmed baking sheet. Broil, turning as needed, until blackened on all sides, about 20 minutes. Using tongs, place the charred pieces in a paper bag and fold the bag to close. Let stand for 10 minutes.

2. In the meantime, heat a dry skillet over medium-high heat. Add the coriander and caraway, and toast, stirring, for 1 minute. Stir in the remaining ½ cup oil and the garlic, and cook for 2 minutes. Transfer the mixture to a blender or food processor.

3. Peel, seed, and chop the blackened peppers and chiles. Add the chopped pepper flesh and the sugar to the mixture in the blender or food processor and pulse to purée. Add salt and black pepper to taste and pulse again.

4. Cool the sauce in the refrigerator, then freeze according to the directions on page 2. The sauce will keep in the freezer for up to 6 months.

5. To serve, follow the directions on page 8 to reheat your sauce, then enjoy it on your choice of base at right.

# HARISSA MEALS TO MAKE

| BASE | QUANTITY | MEAL SUGGESTION |
|------|----------|-----------------|
| (page 10) | ¾ cup sauce per pound of pasta | Toss sauce with penne. Top with a dollop of plain yogurt. Serve with sautéed spinach. |
| (page 12) | ¼ cup sauce per cup of cooked rice | Toss sauce with rice. Top with roasted bell peppers. Serve with green salad. |
| (page 14) | ½ cup sauce per pound of chicken | Toss sauce with chopped chicken. Serve with brown rice and roasted asparagus. |
| (page 15) | ½ cup sauce per pound of shrimp/ scallops | *My Family's Favorite:* Toss sauce with pan-fried scallops. Serve with sliced baguette and steamed artichoke. |
| (page 17) | ½ cup sauce per pound of pork | Toss sauce with shredded pork. Serve with hash browns and tomato salad. |
| (page 18) | ½ cup sauce per pound of beef | Toss sauce with shredded beef. Serve with white rice and sautéed peppers. |
| (page 20) | 2 tablespoons sauce per sandwich | Spread sauce evenly over horizontally sliced baguette. Top with sliced chicken and tomato. |

# CHAPTER 4

# CHEESE AND WINE SAUCES

For me, making a cheese or wine sauce is equivalent to breaking out the big guns. A good cheese sauce is the quickest way to pacify a grumbly, hungry crowd, while a wine sauce adds elegance to any dish with an astonishing lack of effort. All the cheese sauces make excellent dips for appetizers and veggies as well.

# Cheddar Ale

This all-purpose cheese sauce is a hit with kids. For younger kids or anyone who wants a blander sauce, leave out the cayenne pepper. Don't worry about the ale — the alcohol will cook out of the sauce and leave just a bit of flavor behind.

¾ cup (1½ sticks) butter

¾ cup all-purpose flour

6 garlic cloves, minced or pressed

1 heaping tablespoon ground cayenne pepper

Freshly ground black pepper

1½ cups mild ale

1½ cups chicken or vegetable broth

6 cups shredded sharp cheddar cheese

2½ cups half-and-half

1 tablespoon Worcestershire sauce

**1.** Warm the butter in a large saucepan over medium-low heat. Whisk in the flour and cook for 2 to 3 minutes to remove the "floury" taste. Add the garlic, cayenne, and black pepper to taste. Whisk to combine.

**2.** Slowly whisk in the ale and broth, then add the cheese and continue whisking until the sauce is smooth, about 5 minutes. Add the half-and-half and Worcestershire, and reduce the heat to low. Whisk slowly until the sauce is even and hot, 3 to 4 minutes longer.

**3.** Cool the sauce in the refrigerator, then freeze according to the directions on page 2. The sauce will keep in the freezer for up to 1 month.

**4.** To serve, follow the directions on page 8 to reheat your sauce, then enjoy it on any one of the bases on page 136.

*At right: Macaroni with Cheddar Ale sauce*

| BASE | QUANTITY | MEAL SUGGESTION |
|---|---|---|
| (page 10) | 1½ cups sauce per pound of pasta | *My Family's Favorite:* Spoon sauce over macaroni. Serve with sliced red bell peppers and carrot sticks. |
| (page 11) | ⅔ cup sauce per potato | Spoon sauce over potato. Garnish with bacon bits. Serve with green salad. |
| (page 12) | ½ cup sauce per cup of cooked rice | Spoon sauce over rice. Garnish with crushed potato chips. Serve with tomato salad. |
| (page 14) | 1 cup sauce per pound of chicken | Spoon sauce over sliced chicken. Serve with mashed potatoes and sautéed spinach. |
| (page 17) | 1 cup sauce per pound of pork | Spoon sauce over sliced pork. Serve with white rice and roasted beets. |
| (page 18) | 1 cup sauce per pound of beef | Spoon sauce over sliced beef. Serve with sliced baguette and sautéed kale. |
| (page 21) | 3½ cups sauce and 2½ cups vegetable or chicken broth per 4-serving pot | Garnish with crushed potato chips. |

# Gorgonzola Chive Butter

When added to hot food, this compound butter melts instantly into a cheesy sauce. Given the pungency of Gorgonzola and the richness of both cheese and butter combined, a little goes a long way.

2 cups Gorgonzola cheese

1½ cups (3 sticks) butter, at room temperature

12 chives, minced

Salt

**1.** Combine the cheese, butter, chives, and salt to taste in a large mixing bowl and blend thoroughly. Shape into logs on waxed paper, twist the ends closed, and refrigerate until hardened, at least 2 hours. Transfer to freezer containers after the logs have hardened.

**2.** Freeze according to the directions on page 2. Compound butter will keep in the freezer for up to 1 month.

**3.** To serve, follow the directions on page 8 to heat your sauce, then enjoy it on any one of the bases on the next page.

# GORGONZOLA CHIVE BUTTER MEALS TO MAKE

| BASE | QUANTITY | MEAL SUGGESTION |
|---|---|---|
| (page 10) | ¾ cup sauce per pound of pasta | Toss macaroni with sauce. Serve with roasted cauliflower. |
| (page 11) | ⅓ cup sauce per potato | Spoon sauce over potato. Sprinkle with bacon bits. Serve with green salad. |
| (page 12) | ¼ cup sauce per cup of cooked rice | Spoon sauce over rice. Top with diced ham. Serve with steamed green peas. |
| (page 14) | ½ cup sauce per pound of chicken | Spoon sauce over sliced chicken. Serve with sliced baguette and tomato salad. |
| (page 17) | ½ cup sauce per pound of pork | Spoon sauce over sliced pork. Serve with mashed potatoes and roasted asparagus. |
| (page 18) | ½ cup sauce per pound of beef | Spoon sauce over sliced beef. Serve with wild rice blend and roasted carrots. |
| (page 20) | 2 tablespoons sauce per sandwich | *My Family's Favorite:* Spread sauce evenly over sandwich bun. Top with thinly sliced roast beef and chopped fresh parsley. Serve with carrot sticks. |

**At right:** *Roast beef sandwich with Gorgonzola Chive Butter and fresh parsley*

139

# Blue Cheese, Pear, and Hazelnut

MAKES

ABOUT 8 CUPS

Sweet, salty, savory — this sauce has a bit of everything. Try making this one in the fall when pears are at their best. As an uncooked sauce, it can be taken out of the freezer in the morning and defrosted in the refrigerator during the day, then served.

10 ripe pears, peeled, cored, and minced

1½ cups crumbled blue cheese

½ cup (1 stick) butter, at room temperature

1 teaspoon ground nutmeg

2 cups finely chopped hazelnuts

1. Preheat the oven to 350°F/180°C.

2. Combine the pears, blue cheese, butter, and nutmeg in a large mixing bowl and mix thoroughly.

3. Spread the hazelnuts on an ungreased baking sheet and toast in the oven for 5 minutes. Remove from the oven and let cool slightly.

4. Add the cooled hazelnuts to the pear mixture, and stir to combine.

5. Freeze according to the directions on page 2. The sauce will keep in the freezer for up to 1 month.

6. To serve, defrost in the refrigerator and serve cool (as on sandwiches) or *just* warmed up — do not overheat — on your choice of base at right.

# BLUE CHEESE, PEAR, AND HAZELNUT MEALS TO MAKE

| BASE | QUANTITY | MEAL SUGGESTION |
|---|---|---|
| *(page 14)* | I cup sauce per pound of chicken | Spoon sauce over sliced chicken. Serve with biscuits and roasted asparagus. |
| *(page 17)* | I cup sauce per pound of pork | *My Family's Favorite:* Spoon sauce over sliced pork. Serve with mashed potatoes and green salad. |
| *(page 20)* | ¼ cup sauce per sandwich | Spread sauce evenly over sliced sandwich bun. Top with sliced cold pork and crisp lettuce. |

# Cheesy Cashew-Garlic

MAKES

ABOUT 7 CUPS

I love sauces that rely on nuts for their rich flavor and to add protein to a dish, such as this cashew-based alternative to pesto. This rich, pungent sauce can easily be made vegan by substituting a vegan Parmesan for the regular Parmesan, or simply omitting it. I recommend peppering generously for flavor.

4 cups raw cashews, finely chopped

3 cups water

6 garlic cloves, minced or pressed

Generous pinch of salt

¼ cup extra-virgin olive oil

1 cup grated Parmesan cheese

Salt and freshly ground black pepper

1. Combine the cashews and water in a large mixing bowl and let soak for 2 hours (do not drain).

2. Add the garlic and salt to the cashews and blend into a rough paste with an immersion or stand blender, or purée with a food processor.

3. Heat the oil in a large pot over medium-high heat. Add the cashew mixture and cook, stirring often, for 20 minutes. Add the Parmesan and salt and pepper to taste, and cook for 5 minutes longer.

4. Cool the sauce in the refrigerator, then freeze according to the directions on page 2. The sauce will keep in the freezer for up to 6 months.

5. To serve, thaw your sauce in the refrigerator, then enjoy it on your choice of base at right.

# CHEESY CASHEW-GARLIC MEALS TO MAKE

| BASE | QUANTITY | MEAL SUGGESTION |
|---|---|---|
| (page 10) | 1½ cups sauce per pound of pasta | *My Family's Favorite:* Toss sauce with macaroni. Top with shredded carrots. |
| (page 11) | ¾ cup sauce per potato | Top potato with sauce. Serve with green salad. |
| (page 12) | ½ cup sauce per cup of cooked rice | Toss rice with sauce. Top with chopped cashews. Serve with tomato salad. |
| (page 14) | 1 cup sauce per pound of chicken | Spoon sauce over sliced chicken. Serve with sliced baguette and roasted asparagus. |
| (page 17) | 1 cup sauce per pound of pork | Spoon sauce over sliced pork. Serve with pita and roasted Brussels sprouts. |
| (page 18) | 1 cup sauce per pound of beef | Spoon sauce over sliced beef. Serve with French fries and Caesar salad. |

# Pepper Havarti

MAKES

---

ABOUT 8 CUPS

Buttery with hazelnut notes, Havarti just wants to be melted into a luscious sauce. The most "adult" of my cheese sauces, this one is also a good pick for a fondue or appetizer dipping sauce.

1. Warm the butter in a medium saucepan over medium-low heat. Whisk in the flour and cook for 2 to 3 minutes to remove the "floury" taste. Add the garlic, paprika, and pepper. Whisk to combine.

2. Slowly whisk in the milk until the mixture is thoroughly combined. Add the cheese and reduce the heat to low. Cook, whisking often, until the cheese is completely melted and the sauce is smooth, about 10 minutes. Adjust seasonings to taste.

3. Cool the sauce in the refrigerator, then freeze according to the directions on page 2. The sauce will keep in the freezer for up to 1 month.

4. To serve, follow the directions on page 8 to reheat your sauce, then enjoy it on any one of the bases on page 146.

- ¾ cup (1½ sticks) butter
- ¾ cup all-purpose flour
- 8 garlic cloves, minced or pressed
- 1 heaping tablespoon smoked paprika
- 1 tablespoon freshly ground black pepper
- 6 cups milk
- 6 cups grated Havarti cheese

**At right:** *Baked potato topped with Pepper Havarti sauce and roasted garlic*

| BASE | QUANTITY | MEAL SUGGESTION |
|---|---|---|
| (page 10) | 1½ cups sauce per pound of pasta | Spoon sauce over macaroni. Garnish with parsley. Serve with green salad. |
| (page 11) | ⅔ cup sauce per potato | *My Family's Favorite:* Spoon sauce over potato. Garnish with roasted garlic (1 clove per potato). Serve with steamed green beans. |
| (page 12) | ½ cup sauce per cup of cooked rice | Spoon sauce over rice. Sprinkle with additional paprika. Serve with baked winter squash. |
| (page 14) | 1 cup sauce per pound of chicken | Spoon sauce over sliced chicken. Serve with hash browns and sautéed spinach. |
| (page 17) | 1 cup sauce per pound of pork | Spoon sauce over sliced pork. Serve with white rice and steamed peas. |
| (page 18) | 1 cup sauce per pound of beef | Spoon sauce over sliced beef. Serve with mashed potatoes and roasted carrots. |
| (page 20) | ¼ cup sauce per sandwich | Spread sauce evenly over hamburger bun. Top with sliced ham and pan-fried onions. |
| (page 21) | 3½ cups sauce and 2½ cups vegetable broth per 4-serving pot | Garnish with roasted garlic cloves and serve with toasted baguette slices. |

# Caramelized Onion Boursin

MAKES
───────
ABOUT 5 CUPS

This is a good sauce to make while you've got a day's worth of kitchen projects. No matter how long I think it's going to take to caramelize onions, it always seems to take at least a half hour longer. Just do something else and give the onions a stir from time to time without even bothering to mind the clock.

½ cup (1 stick) butter

10 large onions, thinly sliced

½ teaspoon salt

1 (5-ounce) package plain Boursin or other soft cheese

2 cups chicken or vegetable broth

Freshly ground black pepper

**1.** Warm the butter in a large stockpot over low heat. Add the onions and salt, and cook, stirring occasionally, until the onions turn brown and caramelize completely, about 1 hour. If the onions get dry at any point, add water ¼ cup at a time.

**2.** Stir in the Boursin, stock, and pepper to taste. Cover and bring to a simmer, then remove from the heat.

**3.** Cool the sauce in the refrigerator, then freeze according to the directions on page 2. The sauce will keep in the freezer for up to 1 month.

**4.** To serve, follow the directions on page 8 to reheat your sauce, then enjoy it on any one of the bases on page 149.

*Sliced steak with Caramelized Onion Boursin sauce, mushroom rice, and roasted asparagus*

# CARAMELIZED ONION BOURSIN MEALS TO MAKE

| BASE | QUANTITY | MEAL SUGGESTION |
|---|---|---|
| (page 10) | 1½ cups sauce per pound of pasta | Spoon sauce over fusilli. Top with grated Parmesan cheese. Serve with green salad. |
| (page 11) | ⅔ cup sauce per potato | Spoon sauce over potato. Top with grated Parmesan cheese. Serve with sautéed mixed bell peppers. |
| (page 12) | ½ cup sauce per cup of cooked rice | Spoon sauce over rice. Garnish with crumbled bacon. Serve with tomato salad. |
| (page 14) | 1 cup sauce per pound of chicken | Spoon sauce over sliced chicken. Serve with biscuits and sautéed Asian greens. |
| (page 17) | 1 cup sauce per pound of pork | Spoon sauce over sliced pork. Serve with white rice and baby carrots. |
| (page 18) | 1 cup sauce per pound of beef | *My Family's Favorite:* Spoon sauce over sliced beef. Serve with mushroom rice and roasted asparagus. |

## BROWN IS GOOD: CARAMELIZATION

Caramelization is a breakdown of sugars in a food, producing sweetness and a nutty flavor. If you caramelize onions, the sugars in the onions break down from large structures that don't taste sweet to small ones that do. Caramelization happens over low heat and is a long, slow cooking process. If the onions seem dry or are sticking to the bottom of the pan, feel free to add a little water.

Sometimes both caramelization and the Maillard reaction (see page 19) happen in the same foods, and even at the same time. If you sauté onions in butter over low to medium heat, stirring often, they will caramelize and turn brown and sweet. If you fry the same onions in the same butter at a higher heat, they will have a Maillard reaction and turn brown and savory.

# Peppery Red Wine

I love wine sauces for their ability to make a meal more elegant while being secretly economical. They're an excellent way to use the leftovers from last night's bottle of wine, or to use a gifted bottle of wine that is not quite your taste for drinking straight.

6 tablespoons butter

3 large or 6 small shallots, minced

2 heads garlic, cloves minced or pressed

½ teaspoon salt

5 cups beef or mushroom broth

1½ cups red wine

1 heaping teaspoon freshly ground black pepper

1. Warm the butter in a large skillet over medium heat. Add the shallots, garlic, and salt, and sauté until fragrant, 3 to 4 minutes. Add the broth, wine, and pepper, and increase the heat to high. Boil and reduce the sauce, stirring often, for 15 minutes, then remove from the heat.

2. Cool the sauce in the refrigerator, then freeze according to the directions on page 2. The sauce will keep in the freezer for up to 6 months.

3. To serve, follow the directions on page 8 to reheat your sauce, then enjoy it on your choice of base at right.

| BASE | QUANTITY | MEAL SUGGESTION |
|---|---|---|
|  *(page 17)* | 1½ cups sauce per pound of pork | Spoon sauce over sliced pork. Serve with hash browns and sautéed cabbage. |
|  *(page 18)* | 1½ cups sauce per pound of beef | *My Family's Favorite:* Spoon sauce over sliced beef. Serve with baked potatoes and roasted beets. |

# Basil–White Wine

Most fresh herbs are best when freshly chopped, but this is extra true for basil. I recommend waiting until your sauce is being reduced before mincing the basil, so that it goes in the pot no more than 10 minutes after being cut.

½ cup (1 stick) butter

4 large or 8 small shallots, minced

1 teaspoon salt

4 cups white wine

Freshly ground black pepper

1¾ cups half-and-half

1 cup minced fresh basil

1. Warm the butter in a large skillet over medium heat. Add the shallots and salt, and sauté until fragrant, 3 to 4 minutes.

2. Stir in the wine and pepper to taste, and increase the heat to high. Boil and reduce the sauce, stirring often, for 15 minutes.

3. Reduce the heat to low, add the half-and-half, and continue to heat, stirring, for 2 minutes longer. Remove from the heat and stir in the basil.

4. Cool the sauce in the refrigerator, then freeze according to the directions on page 2. The sauce will keep in the freezer for up to 1 month.

5. To serve, follow the directions on page 8 to reheat your sauce, then enjoy it on any one of the bases on the next page.

*At left:* Sliced chicken with Basil– White Wine sauce, baked potato, and roasted eggplant

# BASIL–WHITE WINE MEALS TO MAKE

| BASE | QUANTITY | MEAL SUGGESTION |
|------|----------|-----------------|
| (page 10) | 1½ cups sauce per pound of pasta | Spoon sauce over pasta. Garnish with grated Parmesan cheese. Serve with green salad. |
| (page 11) | ⅔ cup sauce per potato | Spoon sauce over potato. Garnish with grated Parmesan cheese. Serve with roasted asparagus. |
| (page 12) | ½ cup sauce per cup of cooked rice | Spoon sauce over rice. Garnish with grated Parmesan cheese. Serve with baked winter squash. |
| (page 14) | 1 cup sauce per pound of chicken | *My Family's Favorite:* Spoon sauce over sliced chicken. Garnish with chopped fresh basil. Serve with baked potatoes and roasted eggplant. |
| (page 15) | 1 cup sauce per pound of shrimp/scallops | Spoon sauce over pan-fried scallops. Serve with white rice and sautéed green beans. |
| (page 16) | 1 cup sauce per pound of fish | Spoon sauce over pan-fried fillets. Serve with spaghetti and tomato salad. |

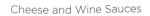

# Tarragon Pecan

The anise-like taste of tarragon is a good partner for mellow pecans in this mild but unforgettable sauce. If you haven't used tarragon before, you'll quickly come to appreciate this French kitchen staple!

1 cup chopped pecans

1 cup grated Asiago cheese

5 ounces (about ½ cup) Boursin or other soft cheese

1 cup chopped fresh tarragon

1 cup (1 stick) butter

3 garlic cloves, minced or pressed

6 shallots, minced

Pinch of salt

3 cups white wine

1 cup heavy cream

**1.** Combine the pecans, Asiago, Boursin, and tarragon in a blender and pulse until well combined. Set the mixture aside.

**2.** Warm the butter in a large skillet over medium-low heat. Add the garlic, shallots, and salt, and sauté, stirring often, until the shallots are soft and cooked through, about 7 minutes. Stir in the wine and increase the heat to high. Boil and reduce the mixture, stirring often, until the liquid is reduced to about I cup, 15 to 20 minutes. Add the cream.

**3.** Reduce the heat to low and add the pecan mixture to the liquid, stirring, until the sauce is hot and completely combined, 5 to 6 minutes.

**4.** Cool the sauce in the refrigerator, then freeze according to the directions on page 2. The sauce will keep in the freezer for up to I month.

**5.** To serve, follow the directions on page 8 to reheat your sauce, then enjoy it on any one of the bases on the next page.

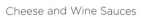

# TARRAGON PECAN MEALS TO MAKE

| BASE | QUANTITY | MEAL SUGGESTION |
|---|---|---|
| (page 10) | 1½ cups sauce per pound of pasta | *My Family's Favorite:* Spoon sauce over rigatoni. Garnish with fresh parsley. Serve with roasted Brussels sprouts. |
| (page 11) | ⅔ cup sauce per potato | Spoon sauce over potato. Garnish with chopped pecans. Serve with green salad. |
| (page 12) | ½ cup sauce per cup of cooked rice | Spoon sauce over rice. Garnish with chopped pecans. Serve with roasted red bell pepper strips. |
| (page 14) | 1 cup sauce per pound of chicken | Spoon sauce over sliced chicken. Serve with macaroni and steamed asparagus. |
| (page 15) | 1 cup sauce per pound of shrimp/ scallops | Spoon sauce over pan-fried scallops. Serve with sliced baguette and steamed green peas. |
| (page 17) | 1 cup sauce per pound of pork | Spoon sauce over sliced pork. Serve with mashed potatoes and braised cabbage. |
| (page 18) | 1 cup sauce per pound of beef | Spoon sauce over sliced beef. Serve with white rice and steamed lima beans. |
| (page 20) | ¼ cup sauce per sandwich | Spread sauce evenly over horizontally sliced baguette. Top with sliced roast beef. |

**At right:** *Rice topped with Tarragon Pecan sauce, chopped pecans, and roasted red pepper strips*

# Rosemary Port

Port is red wine that has had its fermentation process interrupted by the addition of brandy. Rich and sweet, a bit of port makes a nice tipple after dinner. As an ingredient in sauce, it carries a fuller body than red wine and can balance against more robust aromatics, such as the rosemary in this recipe. Rosemary Port sauce is also a good choice to season stronger-tasting meats, such as duck or venison.

6 tablespoons butter

3 large or 6 small shallots, minced

1 teaspoon salt

3 cups beef or mushroom broth

2 cups port

3 tablespoons minced fresh rosemary

**1.** Warm the butter in a large skillet over medium heat. Add the shallots and salt, and sauté until fragrant, 3 to 4 minutes.

**2.** Add the broth and port, and increase the heat to high. Boil and reduce the sauce, stirring often, for 5 minutes. Stir in the rosemary and reduce for 10 minutes longer.

**3.** Cool the sauce in the refrigerator, then freeze according to the directions on page 2. The sauce will keep in the freezer for up to 6 months.

**4.** To serve, follow the directions on page 8 to reheat your sauce, then enjoy it on your choice of base at right.

# ROSEMARY PORT MEALS TO MAKE

| BASE | QUANTITY | MEAL SUGGESTION |
|------|----------|-----------------|
|  *(page 17)* | 1 cup sauce per pound of pork | Spoon sauce over pork slices. Serve with mashed potatoes and sautéed spinach. |
|  *(page 18)* | 1 cup sauce per pound of beef | Spoon sauce over beef slices. Serve with white rice and steamed broccoli. |

## ROSEMARY PORT WITH VENISON

My family's favorite way to enjoy Rosemary Port sauce is over venison medallions. To prepare them, generously butter the outside of the medallions, then sear over high heat in a skillet, flipping halfway through, 2 to 3 minutes per side. Serve with pan-fried potatoes and herbed salad.

# Sherry Cremini

The sophisticated tastes of sherry and cremini mushrooms pair beautifully in this luxurious sauce. The sauce's strong flavor allows it to work particularly well with pasta, especially with a bit of cheese on top, but it's even better with a good steak.

1. Warm the butter in a large skillet over medium-high heat. Add the mushrooms, garlic, and salt, and sauté until browned, 7 to 9 minutes.

2. Season to taste with pepper, stir, and then add the sherry. Reduce the heat to medium-low and cook, stirring, until the sherry evaporates, 15 to 20 minutes. Add the cream and cook, stirring, until the mixture is thick, 6 to 8 minutes.

3. Cool the sauce in the refrigerator, then freeze according to the directions on page 2. The sauce will keep in the freezer for up to 1 month.

4. To serve, follow the directions on page 8 to reheat your sauce, then enjoy it on your choice of base at right.

¾ cup (1½ sticks) butter

8 cups chopped fresh cremini mushrooms

8 garlic cloves, minced or pressed

½ teaspoon salt

Freshly ground black pepper

1 cup sherry

2 cups heavy cream

# SHERRY CREMINI MEALS TO MAKE

| BASE | QUANTITY | MEAL SUGGESTION |
|---|---|---|
| (page 10) | 1½ cups sauce per pound of pasta | *My Family's Favorite:* Spoon sauce over linguine. Garnish with grated Parmesan cheese. Serve with green salad. |
| (page 11) | ⅔ cup sauce per potato | Spoon sauce over potato. Garnish with grated Parmesan cheese. Serve with steamed broccoli. |
| (page 12) | ½ cup sauce per cup of cooked rice | Spoon sauce over rice. Top with shredded mozzarella cheese. Serve with sautéed spinach. |
| (page 17) | 1 cup sauce per pound of pork | Spoon sauce over sliced pork. Serve with baked potato and roasted mixed bell peppers. |
| (page 18) | 1 cup sauce per pound of beef | Spoon sauce over sliced beef. Serve with sliced baguette and roasted carrots. |

# CHAPTER 5

# PESTOS AND SALSAS

Pestos and salsas are two classic types of high-flavor, no-cook sauces. Pesto is renowned for its ability to do well in the freezer, but salsas also do very well. The more finely chopped the fresh ingredients are, the more successfully they will freeze, so don't be afraid to really pulverize them.

# Classic Pesto

Basil is one of those plants that explodes with bounty in the heat of summer. It doesn't dry well or keep long when minced or chopped, but it freezes beautifully in an oil emulsion.

2 cups pine nuts

4 cups finely minced fresh basil

1 cup grated Parmesan cheese

1 cup extra-virgin olive oil

6 garlic cloves, minced or pressed

1 teaspoon salt

1. Preheat the oven to 350°F/180°C.

2. Spread the pine nuts on an ungreased baking sheet and toast in the oven for 5 minutes, or until fragrant and lightly browned. Remove from the oven and let cool slightly.

3. Combine the pine nuts, basil, Parmesan, oil, garlic, and salt in a food processor or blender (or a mixing bowl if using an immersion blender) and pulse or blend until well combined.

4. Freeze according to the directions on page 2. The pesto will keep in the freezer for up to 6 months.

5. To serve, follow the directions on page 8 to heat your pesto, then enjoy it on your choice of base at right.

## OPTIONS FOR MAKING PESTO

Many people think that you need a food processor to make pesto. Happily, they're wrong. Any blender — even a handheld immersion blender, one of my favorite kitchen tools — can make a pesto that, while perhaps slightly rough, tastes fantastic and works well with several bases.

# CLASSIC PESTO MEALS TO MAKE

| BASE | QUANTITY | MEAL SUGGESTION |
|------|----------|-----------------|
| (page 10) | ¾ cup pesto per pound of pasta | *My Family's Favorite:* Toss pesto with angel hair pasta. Top with additional grated Parmesan cheese. Serve with tomato salad. |
| (page 11) | ⅓ cup pesto per potato | Top potato with pesto. Serve with steamed broccoli. |
| (page 12) | ¼ cup pesto per cup of cooked rice | Toss pesto with rice. Top with additional grated Parmesan cheese and pine nuts. Serve with green salad. |
| (page 14) | ½ cup pesto per pound of chicken | Toss pesto with sliced chicken. Serve with linguine and steamed green peas. |
| (page 15) | ½ cup pesto per pound of shrimp/scallops | Toss pesto with hot cooked shrimp or scallops. Serve with rice and sautéed bell peppers. |
| (page 16) | ½ cup pesto per pound of fish | Toss pesto with hot cooked fish. Serve with couscous and sautéed Asian greens. |
| (page 17) | ½ cup pesto per pound of pork | Toss pesto with hot cooked pork. Serve with hash browns and sautéed zucchini. |
| (page 18) | ½ cup pesto per pound of beef | Toss pesto with hot cooked beef. Serve with mashed potatoes and steamed lima beans. |
| (page 20) | 2 tablespoons pesto per sandwich | Spread pesto evenly over bread. Top with sliced turkey and tomato slices. |

# Sun-Dried Tomato Pesto

MAKES

ABOUT 4 CUPS

The rich tang of sun-dried tomatoes makes the flavor of this pesto especially intense. I like to pull out this pesto when I need a pick-me-up before an evening meeting or work session.

**1.** Heat the oil in a large skillet over medium heat. Add the pine nuts and cook for 3 minutes, stirring occasionally. Add the garlic and cook for 2 minutes longer. Remove from the heat and transfer to a blender or the bowl of a food processor.

**2.** Add the tomatoes, basil, vinegar, and salt to the blender or food processor and finely chop. Let the pesto rest for 10 minutes.

**3.** Freeze according to the directions on page 2. The pesto will keep in the freezer for up to 6 months.

**4.** To serve, follow the directions on page 8 to reheat your pesto, then enjoy it on any one of the bases on page 168.

½ cup extra-virgin olive oil

1 cup pine nuts

1 head garlic, cloves minced or pressed

2 cups sun-dried tomatoes packed in oil

¼ cup chopped fresh basil

¼ cup balsamic vinegar

1 teaspoon salt

*At right:* Linguine with Sun-Dried Tomato Pesto

Pestos and Salsas

# SUN-DRIED TOMATO PESTO MEALS TO MAKE

| BASE | QUANTITY | MEAL SUGGESTION |
|---|---|---|
| (page 10) | ¾ cup pesto per pound of pasta | *My Family's Favorite:* Toss pesto with linguine. Top with additional chopped fresh basil. Serve with green salad. |
| (page 11) | ⅓ cup pesto per potato | Top potato with pesto. Serve with steamed broccoli. |
| (page 12) | ¼ cup pesto per cup of cooked rice | Toss pesto with rice. Top with small chunks of ham. Serve with Caesar salad. |
| (page 14) | ½ cup pesto per pound of chicken | Toss pesto with sliced chicken and additional chopped sun-dried tomatoes. Serve with couscous and pan-fried sliced mushrooms. |
| (page 17) | ½ cup pesto per pound of pork | Toss pesto with sliced pork. Serve with French fries and roasted carrots. |
| (page 18) | ½ cup pesto per pound of beef | Toss pesto with sliced beef. Serve with mashed potatoes and steamed artichokes. |
| (page 20) | 2 tablespoons pesto per sandwich | Spread pesto evenly over bread. Top with sliced roast beef and baby spinach. |

# Spinach Pesto

MAKES

ABOUT 5 CUPS

Almonds and spinach make a natural pairing in this delightful version, which is a little lighter on the garlic than most other pestos. Make it in early spring with the first of the baby spinach to celebrate the beginning of green things!

2 cups finely chopped almonds

4 cups finely chopped baby spinach

1 cup grated Parmesan cheese

1 cup extra-virgin olive oil

4 garlic cloves, minced or pressed

1 teaspoon salt

1. Preheat the oven to 350°F/180°C.

2. Spread the almonds on an ungreased baking sheet and toast in the oven for 5 minutes, or until fragrant and lightly browned. Let cool slightly.

3. Combine the almonds, spinach, Parmesan, oil, garlic, and salt in a food processor or blender and pulse until well combined.

4. Freeze according to the directions on page 2. The pesto will keep in the freezer for up to 6 months.

5. To serve, follow the directions on page 8 to heat your pesto, then enjoy it on any one of the bases on page 171.

Pan-fried white fish with
Spinach Pesto, couscous,
and tomato salad

170

| BASE | QUANTITY | MEAL SUGGESTION |
|---|---|---|
| *(page 10)* | ¾ cup pesto per pound of pasta | Toss pesto with linguine. Top with additional grated Parmesan cheese and sliced almonds. Serve with sliced red bell peppers. |
| *(page 11)* | ⅓ cup pesto per potato | Top potato with pesto. Serve with boiled corn on the cob. |
| *(page 12)* | ¼ cup pesto per cup of cooked rice | Toss pesto with rice. Top with additional grated Parmesan cheese and sliced almonds. Serve with Caesar salad. |
| *(page 14)* | ½ cup pesto per pound of chicken | Toss pesto with sliced chicken. Serve with macaroni and steamed carrots. |
| *(page 15)* | ½ cup pesto per pound of shrimp/scallops | Toss pesto with pan-fried shrimp. Serve with white rice and side of sautéed onions and bell peppers. |
| *(page 16)* | ½ cup pesto per pound of fish | *My Family's Favorite:* Spread pesto on pan-fried fillet. Serve with couscous and tomato salad. |
| *(page 17)* | ½ cup pesto per pound of pork | Toss pesto with sliced pork. Serve with mashed potatoes and steamed asparagus. |
| *(page 18)* | ½ cup pesto per pound of beef | Toss pesto with sliced beef. Serve with sliced baguette and steamed artichoke. |
| *(page 20)* | 2 tablespoons pesto per sandwich | Spread pesto evenly over bread. Top with sliced tomatoes and mozzarella cheese. |

# Walnut-Parsley Pesto

MAKES
_____

ABOUT 5 CUPS

You can make a pesto out of virtually any combination of green herbs and nuts or seeds, but some combinations work better than others. Walnuts and parsley make a natural pairing for memorable flavor. This pesto is both richer and slightly more bitter than traditional basil pesto, making it a good winter dish.

2 cups finely chopped walnuts

4 cups lightly packed finely chopped fresh parsley

1 cup grated Parmesan cheese

1 cup extra-virgin olive oil

6 garlic cloves, minced or pressed

1 teaspoon salt

**1.** Preheat the oven to 350°F/180°C.

**2.** Spread the walnuts on an ungreased baking sheet and toast in oven for 5 minutes, or until fragrant and lightly browned. Remove from the oven and let cool slightly.

**3.** Combine the walnuts, parsley, Parmesan, oil, garlic, and salt in a food processor or blender and pulse until well combined.

**4.** Freeze according to the directions on page 2. The pesto will keep in the freezer for up to 6 months.

**5.** To serve, follow the directions on page 8 to heat your pesto, then enjoy it on your choice of base at right.

| BASE | QUANTITY | MEAL SUGGESTION |
|---|---|---|
| *(page 10)* | ¾ cup pesto per pound of pasta | Toss pesto with spaghetti. Top with additional grated Parmesan cheese and toasted walnuts. Serve with steamed green peas. |
| *(page 11)* | ⅓ cup pesto per potato | Top potato with pesto. Serve with tomato salad. |
| *(page 12)* | ¼ cup pesto per cup of cooked rice | Toss pesto with rice. Top with additional grated Parmesan cheese and toasted walnuts. Serve with green salad. |
| *(page 14)* | ½ cup pesto per pound of chicken | Toss pesto with sliced chicken. Serve with couscous and steamed spinach. |
| *(page 16)* | ½ cup pesto per pound of fish | Spread pesto on pan-fried fillet. Serve with wild rice and kale salad. |
| *(page 17)* | ½ cup pesto per pound of pork | Toss pesto with sliced pork. Serve with hash browns and steamed asparagus. |
| *(page 18)* | ½ cup pesto per pound of beef | Toss pesto with sliced beef. Serve with baked potatoes and sautéed mushrooms. |
| *(page 20)* | 2 tablespoons pesto per sandwich | *My Family's Favorite:* Spread pesto evenly over sourdough baguette slices. Top with sliced tomatoes and mozzarella cheese. |

# Mint Pesto

If you like mint sauce on lamb, you'll enjoy this unusual pesto. The mint and pistachios give it a Middle Eastern flair!

**1.** Preheat the oven to 350°F/180°C.

**2.** Spread the pistachios on an ungreased baking sheet and toast in the oven for 5 minutes, or until fragrant and lightly browned. Let cool slightly.

**3.** Combine the pistachios, mint, Parmesan, oil, garlic, and salt in a food processor or blender and pulse until well combined.

**4.** Freeze according to the directions on page 2. The pesto will keep in the freezer for up to 6 months.

**5.** To serve, follow the directions on page 8 to heat your pesto, then enjoy it on your choice of base at right.

- 2 cups finely chopped pistachios
- 4 cups finely chopped fresh mint
- 1 cup grated Parmesan cheese
- 1 cup extra-virgin olive oil
- 6 garlic cloves, minced or pressed
- 1 teaspoon salt

# MINT PESTO MEALS TO MAKE

| BASE | QUANTITY | MEAL SUGGESTION |
|---|---|---|
| (page 10) | ¾ cup pesto per pound of pasta | Toss pesto with linguine. Top with additional grated Parmesan cheese and chopped pistachios. Serve with sautéed sliced red bell peppers. |
| (page 11) | ⅓ cup pesto per potato | Top potato with pesto. Serve with boiled corn on the cob. |
| (page 12) | ¼ cup pesto per cup of cooked rice | Toss pesto with rice. Top with additional grated Parmesan cheese and sliced almonds. Serve with green salad. |
| (page 17) | ½ cup pesto per pound of pork | Toss pesto with sliced pork. Serve with white rice and steamed cauliflower. |
| (page 18) | ½ cup pesto per pound of beef | Toss pesto with sliced beef. Serve with baked potatoes and roasted beets. |
| (page 20) | 2 tablespoons pesto per sandwich | Spread pesto evenly over bread. Top with sliced tomatoes and Havarti cheese. |

## MINT PESTO WITH LAMB

My family's favorite way to enjoy Mint Pesto is tossed with sliced rare lamb. Prepare lamb by cooking a roast at 325°F/165°C to an internal temperature of 135°F/57°C for rare or 145°F/63°C for well done (about 20 minutes per pound). Allow the meat to rest for 30 minutes, then slice. Serve with couscous.

# Tomatillo Salsa Cruda

MAKES

ABOUT 10 CUPS

The bright green color matches the fresh, piquant taste of this south-of-the-border concoction. If you've never prepared fresh tomatillos before, you might be surprised to find that they're sticky beneath their papery husks. The stickiness is one of the plant's defenses against insects, but it is nothing for you to be concerned about. Simply rinse the tomatillos thoroughly before using.

8 cups finely diced fresh tomatillos

2 medium onions, finely chopped

4 jalapeños, minced

1 cup chopped fresh cilantro

½ cup lime juice

2 teaspoons salt

1. Combine the tomatillos, onions, jalapeños, cilantro, lime juice, and salt in a large mixing bowl and mix well. Let rest for 20 minutes to allow the flavors to meld before using or freezing.

2. Freeze according to the directions on page 2. The salsa will keep in the freezer for up to 6 months.

3. To serve, thaw your salsa in the refrigerator, then enjoy it on your choice of base at right.

| BASE | QUANTITY | MEAL SUGGESTION |
|---|---|---|
| *(page 11)* | 1 cup salsa per potato | Spoon salsa over potato. Top with sour cream. Serve with sliced mango. |
| *(page 14)* | 1½ cups salsa per pound of chicken | Spoon salsa over sliced chicken. Serve with warmed tortillas and shredded mozzarella cheese. |
| *(page 15)* | 1½ cups salsa per pound of shrimp/ scallops | Spoon salsa over pan-fried scallops. Serve with white rice and sliced papaya. |
| *(page 17)* | 1½ cups salsa per pound of pork | Spoon salsa over sliced pork. Serve with warmed tortillas and shredded cheddar cheese. |
| *(page 18)* | 1½ cups salsa per pound of beef | Spoon salsa over sliced beef. Serve with tortilla chips and shredded Monterey Jack cheese. |
| *(page 20)* | ⅓ cup salsa per sandwich | *My Family's Favorite:* Spread salsa evenly between two slices of cheese in grilled cheese and ham sandwich. |

# Corn and Chile Salsa

**MAKES**

**ABOUT 13 CUPS**

This salsa is a classic. I recommend using fresh tomatoes and corn only if they are local and picked in season — shipping miles are especially hard on the flavor of tomatoes, and corn sugars start converting to starch the day the corn is picked. If you will be using this salsa within a couple days of making it, you can stir it all together instead of blending.

1. Combine the beans, tomatoes, corn, cilantro, onions, garlic, jalapeños, lime juice, cumin, and salt and pepper to taste in a blender or a large mixing bowl. Pulse lightly in the blender or with an immersion blender. Let rest for 20 minutes to allow the flavors to meld before using or freezing.

2. Freeze according to the directions on page 2. The salsa will keep in the freezer for up to 6 months.

3. To serve, thaw your salsa in the refrigerator, then enjoy it on any one of the bases on the next page.

4 cups cooked black beans

4 cups chopped tomatoes, fresh or canned

3 cups corn, fresh or frozen

1 cup chopped fresh cilantro

2 onions, finely chopped

1 head garlic, cloves minced or pressed

2 jalapeños, minced

½ cup lime juice, fresh or bottled

1 tablespoon ground cumin

Salt and freshly ground black pepper

*At left: Sliced chicken with unblended Corn and Chile Salsa and corn bread*

# CORN AND CHILE SALSA MEALS TO MAKE

| BASE | QUANTITY | MEAL SUGGESTION |
|---|---|---|
| (page 11) | 1 cup salsa per potato | Spoon salsa over potato. Top with ¼ cup shredded cheddar cheese. |
| (page 12) | ¾ cup salsa per cup of cooked rice | Spoon salsa over rice. Top with a dollop of sour cream. |
| (page 14) | 1½ cups salsa per pound of chicken | Spoon salsa over sliced chicken. Serve with corn bread or warmed tortillas and shredded Monterey Jack cheese. |
| (page 15) | 1½ cups salsa per pound of shrimp/scallops | Spoon salsa over pan-fried shrimp. Serve with white rice and sour cream. |
| (page 16) | 1½ cups salsa per pound of fish | Spoon salsa over pan-fried fish fillets. Serve with warmed tortillas and shredded cheddar cheese. |
| (page 17) | 1½ cups salsa per pound of pork | Spoon salsa over sliced pork. Serve with brown rice and shredded mozzarella cheese. |
| (page 18) | 1½ cups salsa per pound of beef | Spoon salsa over sliced beef. Serve with white rice and shredded Monterey Jack cheese. |

## NACHOS

My family's favorite way to enjoy Corn and Chile Salsa is with nachos. Line a rimmed baking sheet with tortilla chips and cover with shredded cheese of your choice. Bake in a 350°F/180°C oven for about 10 minutes, until the cheese melts completely. Serve hot with salsa.

# Mango Salsa

Few recipes capture the riotous bounty of late summer's harvest like this fruity salsa. Pop in a second jalapeño if you prefer more spice, or leave it out altogether if you don't want any.

**1.** Combine the tomatoes, peaches, mangoes, bell peppers, onion, cilantro, lime juice, jalapeño, garlic, and salt in a blender or large mixing bowl. Pulse lightly in the blender or with an immersion blender. Let rest for 20 minutes to allow the flavors to meld before using or freezing.

**2.** Freeze according to the directions on page 2. The salsa will keep in the freezer for up to 6 months.

**3.** To serve, thaw your salsa in the refrigerator, then enjoy it on any one of the bases on page 183.

10 ripe tomatoes, chopped

3 large ripe peaches, peeled and chopped

3 large ripe mangoes, peeled and chopped

2 red bell peppers, seeded and chopped

1 red onion, minced

1½ cups chopped fresh cilantro

¼ cup lime juice

1 jalapeño, minced

3 garlic cloves, minced or pressed

1 teaspoon salt

# MANGO SALSA MEALS TO MAKE

| BASE | QUANTITY | MEAL SUGGESTION |
|---|---|---|
| (page 14) | 1½ cups salsa per pound of chicken | Spoon salsa over sliced chicken. Serve with white rice and green salad. |
| (page 15) | 1½ cups salsa per pound of shrimp/scallops | Spoon salsa over pan-fried shrimp. Serve with whole-wheat tortillas. |
| (page 16) | 1½ cups salsa per pound of fish | Spoon salsa over pan-fried fillets. Serve with white rice and carrot sticks. |
| (page 17) | 1½ cups salsa per pound of pork | Spoon salsa over sliced pork. Serve with tortillas and sour cream. |
| (page 18) | 1½ cups salsa per pound of beef | Spoon salsa over sliced beef. Serve with coconut rice and green salad. |
| (page 20) | ⅓ cup salsa per sandwich | *My Family's Favorite:* Spread soft Mexican white cheese or cream cheese evenly over tortillas. Toss salsa with shrimp and use as stuffing to make summer shrimp burritos. |

**At left:** *Shrimp and Mango Salsa burritos*

# Tomatillo Avocado

The bright, rhubarby tang of tomatillos plays against the rich creaminess of avocados to make an immensely satisfying no-cook sauce that is particularly refreshing on hot summer days. Defrost it in the refrigerator during the day and enjoy it cold or at room temperature. We call it "green goodness"!

3 cups chopped fresh tomatillos

3 large ripe avocados

3 jalapeño, serrano, or similar chiles (optional)

¾ cup chopped fresh cilantro

⅓ cup lime juice

Salt

1. Combine the tomatillos, avocados, chiles (if using), cilantro, lime juice, and salt to taste in a blender or large mixing bowl. Pulse lightly in the blender or with an immersion blender. Let rest for 20 minutes to allow the flavors to meld before using or freezing.

2. Freeze according to the directions on page 2. The salsa will keep in the freezer for up to 6 months.

3. To serve, thaw your salsa in the refrigerator, then enjoy it cold or at room temperature on your choice of base at right.

| BASE | QUANTITY | MEAL SUGGESTION |
|------|----------|-----------------|
| (page 11) | ⅔ cup salsa per potato | Spoon salsa over potato. Top with shredded cheddar cheese. Serve with carrot sticks. |
| (page 14) | 1 cup salsa per pound of chicken | Spoon salsa over sliced chicken. Serve with white rice and green salad. |
| (page 15) | 1 cup salsa per pound of shrimp/scallops | Spoon salsa over pan-fried scallops. Serve with tortillas and Caesar salad. |
| (page 16) | 1 cup salsa per pound of fish | Spoon salsa over pan-fried fillets. Serve with tortilla chips and steamed spinach. |
| (page 17) | 1 cup salsa per pound of pork | Spoon salsa over sliced pork. Serve with white rice and tomato salad. |
| (page 18) | 1 cup salsa per pound of beef | Spoon salsa over sliced beef. Serve with mashed potatoes and steamed zucchini. |
| (page 20) | ¼ cup salsa per sandwich | *My Family's Favorite:* Spread salsa evenly over a tortilla. Top with sliced pork and Monterey Jack cheese. Roll to make a wrap. |

# More Flavor Enhancers

## COMPOUND BUTTERS

A homemade compound butter is one of my favorite ways to dress up just about anything on the quick. Impressive at the table yet easy to make, compound butters store well in the refrigerator or freezer. I've included a few classic recipes for you to try, but I encourage you to experiment with making your own as well. Consider adding lemon juice or a flavored vinegar, garlic or shallots, or any spices you like.

If you are vegan or just want to experiment with another flavored cooking oil, try using virgin coconut oil in place of butter. Choose ingredients that complement the coconut flavor, such as ginger, curry, cardamom, and lime.

### Herb Butter

Herb butter is one of the most efficient and rewarding ways to make the most of your fresh herbs. Put it on toast, baked potatoes, pasta, rice, corn on the cob, or nearly any other savory food. If you want to be fancy, use a mold to make a pretty shaped butter.

---

#### MAKES ¾ CUP

---

- ½ cup (1 stick) salted butter, at room temperature
- ½ cup minced herbs (basil, cilantro, dill, parsley, rosemary, thyme, or a combination)
- 1 tablespoon white wine vinegar

Place the butter, herbs, and vinegar in a medium mixing bowl and mix with a fork until evenly combined. Transfer the butter to a large piece of waxed paper. Roll into a log and twist the ends of the paper to close. Refrigerate until solid, about 3 hours. Butter will keep in the refrigerator for up to 5 days, or in the freezer for up to 1 month. Cut the butter into pats when ready to use.

## Café de Paris Butter

A generous pat of this butter, which was first developed in Geneva (not Paris!), is traditionally served on top of a steak. It's also excellent on most other meats and seafood.

MAKES ABOUT 1 CUP

½ cup (1 stick) salted butter, at room temperature

2 tablespoons extra-virgin olive oil

1 tablespoon Dijon mustard

1 tablespoon tomato paste

1 teaspoon lemon juice

½ teaspoon smoked paprika

½ teaspoon curry powder

1 shallot, minced

¼ cup minced fresh chives

1 teaspoon minced fresh thyme

Salt and freshly ground black pepper

Place the butter, oil, mustard, tomato paste, lemon juice, paprika, curry powder, shallot, chives, thyme, and salt and pepper to taste in a medium mixing bowl and mix with a fork until evenly combined. Transfer the butter to a large piece of waxed paper. Roll into a log and twist the ends of the paper to close. Refrigerate until solid, about 3 hours. Butter will keep in the refrigerator for up to 5 days, or in the freezer for up to 1 month. Cut the butter into pats when ready to use.

## Better Chicken Butter

Slip pats of this butter right under the skin of a whole chicken before you roast it. I also love it added to plain white rice or a baked potato.

MAKES ABOUT 1 CUP

1 cup (2 sticks) salted butter, at room temperature

2 tablespoons shiitake mushroom powder

1 tablespoon minced fresh parsley

1 tablespoon minced fresh thyme

2 garlic cloves, minced or pressed

1 tablespoon lemon juice

Salt and freshly ground black pepper

Place the butter, mushroom powder, parsley, thyme, garlic, lemon juice, and salt and pepper to taste in a medium mixing bowl and mix with a fork until evenly combined. Transfer the butter to a large piece of waxed paper. Roll into a log and twist the ends of the paper to close. Refrigerate until solid, about 3 hours. Butter will keep in the refrigerator for up to 5 days, or in the freezer for up to 1 month. Cut the butter into pats when ready to use.

## Cinnamon Butter

This sweet and spicy compound butter is just right for toast or waffles.

MAKES ABOUT ½ CUP

- ½ cup (1 stick) salted butter, at room temperature
- 2 tablespoons honey
- 1 tablespoon ground cinnamon

Place the butter, honey, and cinnamon in a medium mixing bowl and mix with a fork until evenly combined. Transfer the butter to a large piece of waxed paper. Roll into a log and twist the ends of the paper to close. Refrigerate until solid, about 3 hours. Butter will keep in the refrigerator for up to 5 days, or in the freezer for up to 1 month. Cut the butter into pats when ready to use.

# FLAVORED SALTS

One of the easiest and quickest ways to add zest to a simple dish is to add a flavored salt. There are any number of flavored salts and specialty salts on the market, but you can easily reproduce them at home at a fraction of the cost and in about no time flat. Plus, salts made with fresh ingredients at home are much more flavorful than their commercial counterparts made with dried herbs.

## Herb Salt

You can use almost any combination of herbs you like for this recipe. Try a summery blend of basil, chives, and cilantro, or a wintery combination of oregano, parsley, and thyme.

MAKES ABOUT 1 CUP

- ½ cup table salt
- 1 cup stemmed and roughly chopped fresh herbs (such as basil, chives, cilantro, oregano, parsley, or thyme)

Combine the salt and herbs on a cutting board and mince, continually mixing them together as you work the knife. Spread the mixture on a baking sheet and leave in a warm, dry place, stirring occasionally, until completely dry, 2 to 3 days. Store the salt in tightly sealed containers in a cool, dark place. Salt will keep in an airtight container for up to 1 year.

## Rosemary Lemon Salt

This attractive flavored salt is wonderful on chicken, roasted vegetables, baked potatoes, and even popcorn.

MAKES ABOUT 1 CUP

1 cup table salt

3 tablespoons minced fresh rosemary

Zest and juice of 1 lemon

1. Preheat the oven to 200°F/95°C. Line a baking sheet with parchment paper and set aside.

2. Combine the salt, rosemary, and lemon zest and juice in a small mixing bowl, or, if a finer consistency is desired, pulse in a food processor.

3. Transfer the salt mixture to the prepared baking sheet and spread in a single, thin, even layer. Place in the oven and bake for 20 minutes, or until dry.

4. Remove from the oven and let cool for 5 minutes. Break up any lumps by hand, then place in containers and seal tightly with secure lids. Wait at least a day before using. Salt will keep in an airtight container for up to 1 year.

## Spruce Bud Salt

This is one of the more unusual salts I make, and it's also one of my favorites. To prepare it, I harvest the small, tender, pale green buds of new needle growth from spruce trees. I use the tips from buds that are exposed but still closed or just beginning to open. This seasoning is great on scallops, chicken, beef, and venison.

MAKES ABOUT 1 CUP

½ cup spruce bud tips, finely minced

¾ cup table salt

Mix the spruce bud tips with the salt in a large shallow pan. Let dry at room temperature, uncovered, stirring a couple of times a day, until the flavored salt is completely dry, about 2 days. Store in a tightly sealed container. Salt will keep in an airtight container for up to 1 year.

# Meal Planner

Go to storey.com/meal-planner/ to download and print out the meal planner below. It will help you plan out the week ahead and organize your grocery shopping. Stick the planner on the fridge door for an easy reminder and to let everyone know what to expect for dinner!

## Dinner Menus

### MONDAY
Sauce
Base
Extras

### TUESDAY
Sauce
Base
Extras

### WEDNESDAY
Sauce
Base
Extras

### THURSDAY
Sauce
Base
Extras

### FRIDAY
Sauce
Base
Extras

### SATURDAY
Sauce
Base
Extras

### SUNDAY
Sauce
Base
Extras

### NOTES

# Metric Conversion Charts

Unless you have finely calibrated measuring equipment, conversions between US and metric measurements will be somewhat inexact. It's important to convert the measurements for all of the ingredients in a recipe to maintain the same proportions as the original.

## WEIGHT

| To convert | to | multiply |
|---|---|---|
| ounces | grams | ounces by 28.35 |
| pounds | grams | pounds by 453.5 |
| pounds | kilograms | pounds by 0.45 |

## TEMPERATURE

| To convert | to | |
|---|---|---|
| Fahrenheit | Celsius | subtract 32 from Fahrenheit temperature, multiply by 5, then divide by 9 |

## VOLUME

| To convert | to | multiply |
|---|---|---|
| teaspoons | milliliters | teaspoons by 4.93 |
| tablespoons | milliliters | tablespoons by 14.79 |
| fluid ounces | milliliters | fluid ounces by 29.57 |
| cups | milliliters | cups by 236.59 |
| cups | liters | cups by 0.24 |
| pints | milliliters | pints by 473.18 |
| pints | liters | pints by 0.473 |
| quarts | milliliters | quarts by 946.36 |
| quarts | liters | quarts by 0.946 |
| gallons | liters | gallons by 3.785 |

# Index

Page numbers in *italic* indicate photos of bases.

# STOCK UP ON KITCHEN CREATIVITY
## WITH MORE BOOKS FROM STOREY

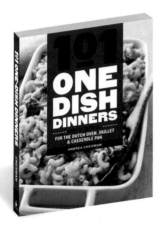

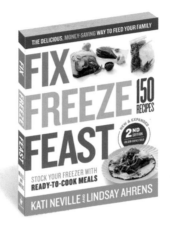

**by Andrea Chesman**
Get a balanced dinner on the table in a single dish! These recipes include classic baked meals like chicken potpie and lasagna, as well as diverse stovetop suppers like jambalaya and seafood paella, plus plenty of soups and hearty salads.

**by Kati Neville & Lindsay Ahrens**
Cook one bulk recipe and feed a family of four for three nights. With these 150 make-ahead meals — including traditional favorites like Chicken Parmigiana and Tomato-Basil Soup plus delectable delights such as Moroccan Meatballs and Lemon-Blueberry Strata — there's something for everyone.

**by Olwen Woodier**
Liven up your cooking with an array of simple pestos, pastes, and purées that use just a few fresh ingredients and showcase flavors from around the globe. An additional 75 recipes encourage you to incorporate pestos into every meal.